BR

ALLPRODAD®

PLAY
OF THE
DAY

BRYAN R. DAVIS

PLAY OF THE DAY

LIVING INK BOOKS™
Writing Worth Reading™

HARD-HITTING DAILY THOUGHTS FOR DADS

Play of the Day

Copyright © 2004 by Bryan R. Davis
Published by Living Ink Books, an imprint of AMG Publishers
6815 Shallowford Rd.
Chattanooga, Tennessee 37421

ISBN 0-89957-151-4

First printing—March 2004
Cover designed by Daryle Beam, Market Street Design, Inc.
    Chattanooga, Tennessee
Cover picture of Tony Dungy provided courtesy of the Indianapolis
    Colts, taken by A. J. Macht
Interior design and typesetting by Reider Publishing Services,
    West Hollywood, California
Edited and Proofread by Jonathan Wright, Dan Penwell,
    Sharon Neal, and Warren Baker

Printed in Canada.
10 09 08 07 06 05 04 –T– 8 7 6 5 4 3 2 1

To my wife, Christy.
You're a true treasure from heaven.
Your love is the backdrop of everything written here.

To Mom and Dad.
Thanks for a parenting job well done.
This book exemplifies all you have taught me.

To Jeremy.
I couldn't be prouder of my little bro.
By the way, I need help moving this weekend.

Soli Deo gloria!

CONTENTS

Football is not an easy game to play or coach. Out on the field, emotions can run so high that players and coaches do make mistakes. The game is so fast-paced that a moment's slip in concentration can have devastating consequences. Weather conditions play a big factor in coaching strategy as well as the friendliness or hostility of the fans. What separates winning teams and coaches from the rest is the ability to execute a game plan no matter what situations they encounter.

The same is true in fatherhood. Work stress, financial pressures, and cultural mores can cause even the best dad to deviate from a tried-and-true family game plan. A lapse in focus by a father is devastating for his family. But how can dads be motivated and informed on being better parents? I believe *Play of the Day* provides the answers to both of these essentials.

We at Family First started the ALL-PRO DAD program because we believe our nation needs fathers who are educated and equipped to do their most important job—being good fathers. From a daily e-mail service to online articles to interactive surveys, ALL-PRO DAD and its website (www.allprodad.com) exist to serve fathers and to help them as they struggle to be the best dads they can. This book, *Play of the Day,* is the next step we're taking to be the ultimate resource in fathering. We trust you'll find the ideas in these pages to be of great benefit to you and your family. Please join our team and make ALL-PRO DAD a part of your daily life. I believe you and your family will benefit greatly.

—Tony Dungy, National Football League
Head Coach 2002–2003—Indianapolis Colts;
1996–2001—Tampa Bay Buccaneers;
Defensive Coordinator and Defensive Back
Coach 1992–1995—Minnesota Vikings;
1989–1991—Kansas City Chiefs;
1981–1988—Pittsburgh Steelers

This book is written on a simple premise—the fact that your kids need you. They need you to be involved in their lives, they need you to respect their mother, and they need you to love them. If you do those three things well, you're on your way to being an all-pro dad.

Play of the Day is not primarily about football players—though we're grateful that they're willing to be involved in our cause. *Play of the Day* is written for fathers in all walks of life. It's written for the dad who is heavily involved in his kids' lives as well as for the one who hasn't seen his children in over a decade. In other words, it's written to help all men improve their relationship with their kids no matter what their past may be.

Time is fleeting. Our lives are a vapor—here today, gone tomorrow. With every day we've borrowed, we have an obligation to live it wisely. And that means a priority on raising children the best we know how. So we've developed this resource to give you our best thoughts and ideas on how you can do your most important job well.

I thank you for the honor of using *Play of the Day* to help strengthen your family. I pray that its contents will turn the hearts of fathers and children toward each other. And please don't hesitate to contact us here at ALL-PRO DAD if we can assist you in any way.

—Bryan R. Davis

ACKNOWLEDGMENTS

I wish to express my thanks to the entire staff of *Family First* for all their help and support. This book would not have been possible without you. I'd also like to extend my appreciation to all the faithful donors of *Family First* who have stood by us year in and year out. Thank you for helping us to reach fathers and families.

I especially would like to recognize Coach Tony Dungy, Coach Clyde Christensen, and all the National Football League players who make ALL-PRO DAD what it is. It takes courage to play and coach football. It takes greater courage to be a good father. You are the role models our country so desperately needs.

Thanks to the The National Center for Fathering (NCF) for the use of your invaluable material. Your website, www.fathers.com, is a remarkable source for dads to find information and practical ideas for nearly every fathering situation.

And thank you to Dan Penwell and the entire staff at AMG Publishers, who have been so easy to work with. You all have made a dream come true.

Finally, I wish to express my appreciation to the editors and proofreaders who worked closely with the manuscript to give it the ultimate in professionalism: Jonathan Wright, Sharon Neal, and Warren Baker.

Do Your Children Operate on CST?

Having trouble getting Junior to come in after playing outside or staying in his bed when he should be going to sleep? Kids operate on CST—Children Standard Time. In other words, when you want your son or daughter to do something or stop doing something right now, it seems to take forever for your wishes to register with them. But it doesn't have to be that way.

You can implement a new rule:

FOR EVERY MINUTE THAT YOUR SON OR DAUGHTER PROCRASTINATES WHEN YOU TELL HIM OR HER TO DO SOMETHING, THEY LOSE FIVE MINUTES OF THEIR FREE TIME.

As an example: If they don't do a chore, or they don't come inside, or they don't obey in any number of other ways, they are penalized five minutes for each minute of procrastination. Five minutes of procrastination could be translated into missing twenty-five minutes of television free time or twenty-five minutes of free time on the computer. You can use the phrase "the clock is ticking," and they'll know they're being penalized. You'll be amazed how suddenly they hear and react.

Are You an Indirect Criticizer?

A New Orleans Saints general manager, when asked after a loss what he thought of the refs, stated, "I'm not allowed to comment on lousy officiating."

His comment was geared to be inflammatory while allegedly observing proper protocol. The same is true for dads. A lot of times we make statements that are hurtful even when we don't raise our voice or directly criticize. Make sure what you say is ultimately encouraging your child to become a better person—not aiming to tear them down—because in the end, we're all on the same team.

Talking to Kids about Death

One of the challenges in being a father is to try to explain something to children who have not had that particular life experience. Such is the case with the passing of a loved one. When a beloved relative or friend dies, it's very difficult to explain to kids, during the grieving process, why this person had to "go away." So when your children are old enough, maybe 6–8 years old, talk to them about death before a loved one dies. Let them know that death is a natural part of life. This will open the door to talk about faith, love, and the value of living each moment wisely.

Remember Being Bullied in School?

It was usually done by a guy named Spike who had a flat-top and was about twenty pounds overweight. And while you may look back at that time with a little bit of amusement, it was probably fairly traumatic for you then. Well, certain things don't change over time. Studies show that one of the major issues children want to talk about with their fathers is the matter of bullying and teasing. It can be dreadful going to school when there's someone continually intimidating them. So be sure to bring up that subject with your children, and let them know what they can do when that situation arises—namely, confide in you.

Are Your Kids Answering Your Questions with One-Word Replies?

You ask them how they're doing, and they say "Fine." You ask them how school is going, and they say "Good." Don't let your children get away with that type of response. Kids hit an age when they want to answer your questions with the least thought or effort possible. And if you allow them to give one-word answers, communication will drop off dramatically. So keep prodding and poking, even if it annoys them a little. Communication is the key to being a successful parent, and successful communication is always two-way communication.

Authority Seems to Be Off Our Radar

I was half-listening to the radio the other night when an ad suddenly grabbed my attention. It was for a radar detection system for the car so I could determine if a police officer was clocking my speed. The tag line said it was "the only way to avoid costly speeding tickets." I thought to myself, *No, it's not. I could just go the speed limit.*

It's amazing how that option wasn't even considered by the advertiser. I also thought how it appears to children when their dads recklessly speed, joke about fudging numbers on tax returns, or bring home office supplies for personal use. Little peccadilloes by fathers can instill in their kids disrespect for authority.

So before you lecture your son or daughter again on why they should obey you, look at your own life to see if you're obeying the law yourself. Practice what you preach.

Side Benefits of Being an Engaged Father

Fatherhood expert Ken Canfield of The National Center for Fathering writes:

> During those first few years of his child's life, a father will bond and establish a relationship with his child which will affect the well-being of both. The benefits to the child are well documented, but what's in it for the dad? Joseph Pleck's research shows that a father who dares to become involved in his child's birth and early child-rearing is less likely to suffer an accidental and premature death, be admitted to a hospital, have contact with the law, and be involved in substance abuse. He is also likely to have a greater overall sense of well-being. Engaged fathering has its rewards.
>
> © 2000 by The National Center for Fathering

Well said, Dr. Canfield. Well said.

Fighting the Sands of Time

If you're like most men, you have a wife desperately trying to hold on to her youth. She has a vast assortment of creams, vitamins, and books all on maintaining her beauty. She may even lay a few cucumber peels on her eyes. And you thought they were only good for salads. It's important to remember that feeling pretty is a big deal to women. It's why they shop for clothes for hours. A lot of how they view themselves is how they perceive others view them.

So what are you doing to encourage your wife? When is the last time you told her she was beautiful? Don't just assume she knows it. Make sure you tell her that specifically when you go home tonight. It's a compliment she'll treasure and well worth a few extra cucumbers.

Don't Let Your Kids Get Caught in the Crossfire

When you and your spouse have a passionate disagreement—where you handle it is just as important as how you handle it. Don't argue in front of your kids. It makes children uneasy when they sense conflict between adults. Instead, if you want to discuss things further, do it away from your children. Let your kids see teamwork, not tension, in their family life.

Have You Considered Reading with Your Wife?

Have you considered taking time to read with your wife? No, that doesn't mean having her look over your shoulder while you're reading a motorcycle magazine. I mean you and your wife both reading the same book, then getting together to discuss the contents.

Charles Eliot said in his book *The Durable Satisfactions of Life,* "Books are the quietest and most constant of friends; they are the most accessible and wisest of counselors, and the most patient of teachers." In other words, books can be great marriage counselors! Find a helpful book on marriage, faith, life stories, or any of a host of other topics. Pick a book whose chapters aren't too long. This allows you to both read a chapter a week and discuss the contents over breakfast. And take the initiative in selecting the book. It will be time well spent.

Bosses vs. Wives

Let's say you had an employee who, whenever you spoke to him or her, averted eye contact and made alien grunts and gestures that no one could interpret. Such an employee probably wouldn't be working long for you, right?

Now, how many similarities can you draw between this deadbeat employee and the way you interact with your wife? When she speaks to you, do you make eye contact? And rather than answering her questions, do you make strange noises and exasperations? Far too many men are much more sociable with their bosses than their wives. No wonder there's so much marital friction. So treat your wife with the respect you treat your boss. Better yet, treat her *better*.

What? Shop with My Wife?

It's no mystery that most women enjoy the shopping experience. And if you're like most men, you shop with the "hunter" mentality—to get what you need as quickly as possible and then get back to the cave. Shopping with your wife can tend to frustrate this plan of yours. Instead, look at shopping with your wife as another way to spend top-quality time with her. When you go shopping with her, have the idea in mind to use this opportunity for communication, not just material accumulation. And spending time together will be the greatest gift of all.

Recollections of the First Date

One of the keys to a great marriage is a healthy dose of surprise every once in a while. One great thing to do tonight after dinner is telling your wife some things about you that she may not know. Try recalling some of the fun times when you first started dating. If you can remember what she was wearing on your first date or where you went, she's really going to enjoy that. She may also like hearing about how nervous you might have been—and how you feared throwing up at any time. And to put the icing on the cake, tell her when you first knew you were in love with her.

Do You Have a Picture of Your Wife on Your Desk at Work?

Keeping a photograph of your wife on your desk may sound a little hokey, but really, it's a great idea. *Number one,* it will hopefully serve as a constant reminder of the importance she plays in all areas of your life, even your work! *Number two,* having a picture of her will open up conversation with your fellow coworkers and customers as they ask about her and will hopefully give you the opportunity to encourage them to be more marriage-centered. So place that picture of your wife on your desk—and show the world what a princess you married!

Use Mystery to Make Family History

If you have younger kids, take them on a mystery event. It's simple to pull off, and it's been a real hit in a lot of families. Tell the kids that next Saturday you will all be doing something together, but don't tell them what it is. The excitement about the unknown event and the incentive to behave are very palpable during the week. Then take them on a simple but fun trip, such as fishing or miniature golfing. But the anticipation is what really makes it fun. And if the event doesn't turn out exactly as you planned, the kids don't know, and you don't have to deal with a lot of complaints—so it's no mystery why Dad loves these events too!

Sending Love from Home to Homeroom

Consider sending a note to your kids that they'll read sometime during the school day. The note can be as simple as wishing them well on a test they'll be taking or encouraging them as they prepare for an after-school sporting game. Or you can just remind them how much you love them and why they're so special. Slip the notes into their textbooks or lunch bags. It will be a great way to connect with your kids even when you're not right there with them.

Do You Have a Video or Pictures of Your Wedding?

When's the last time you saw the video or photograph album of your wedding? When's the last time you showed them to your children? Your kids will love seeing Mom feeding cake to Dad or seeing Dad in a tux with a mullet haircut. But even more important, they'll experience the moment when you all pledged your love for each other and realize the significance of it. So dust off the wedding videos and pictures. You'll get a great conversation going with your kids about the importance of lifetime love.

A Special Drawer
May Be the Answer

Author Stephanie Thurrott has a great idea:

> I'll be honest. I love the way my living room looks
> when it's free of toys. But I also know that my son is
> likely to turn on the TV when he walks in, since
> there's nothing else to catch his attention. My solu-
> tion? A drawer of his own in an end table, filled with
> watercolors and brushes, washable markers and
> crayons, Play-Doh®, rubber stamps, and construction
> paper. He can make surprises for Daddy or just learn
> how colors blend as he mixes Play-Doh® together.

Beats just plopping down in front of the television,
doesn't it?

Want to Save Some Serious
Money at the Grocery Store?

You can do more to save money at the grocery than just
clipping coupons. Here's the trick—shop a month in
advance at a deep discount grocery store. Some families'
food bills have been cut as much as half by doing so. The
real savings isn't so much buying large quantities at once,
although that helps, but forcing you and your wife to plan
your meals out in advance so there aren't a lot of last-
minute rushes to a restaurant or picking up take-out meals.
It really works!

Is Your House a Scene of Organized Chaos?

Controlled chaos is a family pattern that's very easy to fall into. In fact, it's what will happen unless you take steps to avoid it. Now most of us cannot have the pre-packaged "Leave It to Beaver" family organization. But there *is* one important suggestion I can offer—a family devotional time. This is a time set aside each day when all members of the family are required to be there. Of course, this isn't ironclad, but it's a general guideline.

Then you as a father take the lead in sharing important things with your family. And don't worry—you don't need to wear a cardigan vest to have a successful conversation.

Want a Fun Way to Find Out What Your Children Are Thinking?

To get a glimpse inside your children's minds, play "three wishes." It's as simple as it sounds. Ask them to tell you what they would ask for if they had three wishes. When they answer, talk about what they chose—even if it's something as basic as a new dog. You might find out that your children have hopes and dreams you can help them achieve. Or you might learn that there's something painful in their life they need your help changing. So if you've been wishing for a way to get your children to open up, give this idea a try.

Good News about Kids and Smoking

According to a recent issue of *Group* magazine, the number of smoking kids has plummeted over the past five years. The percentage of eighth graders who smoke has dropped by 43 percent over the last five years. The drop is 30 percent for high school sophomores and 19 percent for seniors. There are two main reasons for this. First are the antismoking campaigns. University of Michigan researcher, Lloyd Johnston, says about these campaigns, "There really is an attitudinal shift going on, with more young people saying that they see smoking as dangerous."

The second reason is parental relationships. A new study by Dartmouth Medical School reveals that teenagers who think their parents would be very upset if they started smoking are far less likely to do it. Psychologist Joseph Allen says that kids will "defer to their peers on taste in music and clothes, but for serious decisions about their lives, they look to their parents more." It's another encouraging example of the power that parents have in their children's' lives.

Buckling Up Is the Manly Thing to Do

Dads aren't usually known to be very strong advocates of having their kids buckle seat belts. This is especially the case on short trips in the car. But according to the National Safe Kids Campaign, 75 percent of all crashes occur within twenty-five miles of home. And most of those take place on roads with maximum speed limits of forty miles per hour or less. The Insurance Institute for Highway Safety reports that motor vehicle crashes account for one in three injury-related deaths among children. Further, it states that crash injuries are the leading cause of death among five- to twelve-year-olds.

So take the couple seconds necessary to buckle your kids up. And set the example by buckling up yourself. It's not only logical—in most states it's the law as well.

A Safety Plan for Your Clan

Do you have a home safety plan or a checklist of things to be aware of to prevent harm to your family? Some examples include installing smoke detectors on each floor and changing the batteries each year, checking cords for exposed wiring and fraying, and placing cribs away from windows, window blinds, and curtain cords. Look online to find web sites with a home safety checklist, and print the list out. You can never be too safe when it comes to your family.

Shaken Baby Syndrome
Is Far Too Common

It's 3:00 AM. Your newborn is crying again. Your wife is frazzled after being up two straight nights caring for your little one. You've had a hard time sleeping as well. Work has been especially hectic lately, only adding to your stress level. So with quite a bit of frustration, you get up and try to attend to your baby. But your infant keeps crying and crying—and your anger keeps mounting and mounting. It's at this point that you may be most vulnerable to shaking your baby too hard in order to get him or her to quiet down.

Nearly 50,000 cases of shaken baby syndrome occur each year in the United States, and adult males in their twenties who are the baby's father or mother's boyfriend are typically those who are guilty of the shaking. Most shaking occurs in situations similar to those described above, so be aware of how easily stress and frustration can lead to a breaking point. And if you find yourself way over your head, seek help at a local church or government agency. There's plenty of help if you need it.

The Sum of All Fears: Visiting the Doctor

Did you know that on average, women consult physicians 30 percent more often than men do? Now, dads, we know why that is. We don't like going to doctors, because we may see that as a sign of weakness—an acknowledgment that we need help. In addition, we don't like to think there's anything wrong with us and don't want to be at anyone else's mercy. But we do need to see doctors on a regular basis, not just for our sake but for our families' sake as well. Even if you feel fine, early detection of diseases caught by standard tests can make all the difference in the world.

So go ahead and set up that physical you've been putting off for years. Your life and your family's well-being may depend on it.

Can Exercising Help You Become a Better Parent?

Exercising can actually help make you a better father. Proper exercise can help reduce stress—meaning that you're less likely to blow up at your kids. It will also give you energy and stamina to keep up with your children. You know better than I do that your young ones are little packets of energy, and you need all the strength you can get as you scurry after them. Exercise can also help you share time with your wife if you designate certain days and times of the week for both of you to participate.

Germ Warfare

Did you know that a few simple steps you can take in the bathroom would cut down on the amount of germs your kids are exposed to? First, of course, make sure your kids wash their hands as much as possible with hot water and soap. There simply is no better substitute for good health than hand washing. Change your kids' toothbrushes on a regular basis—even if the toothbrush doesn't show much wear. That's another major germ source. Teach your kids to flush the toilet with the lid down. Many germs get sprayed into the air when flushing occurs with the lid up. Also, make sure they scrub the sinks, toilets, and shower with bleach or another good cleaning agent, and mop the floors. A clean bathroom is essential to keeping your kids healthy. And having the bathroom smell better is always a great benefit as well.

"Being a good quarterback takes determination, dedication, and perseverance. Those are also the qualities you need to be a good father. ALL-PRO DAD shows men how to develop those qualities."

—Mark Brunell, Quarterback 2004—Washington Redskins; 1995–2003—Jacksonville Jaguars; 1994—Green Bay Packers

All-pro quarterback Mark Brunell is also an all-pro dad. While Mark was growing up, his dad played an integral role in his life, as he still does today. Dave Brunell was the athletic director at the high school where Mark excelled in football, basketball, and baseball. Dave was always encouraging and very supportive of Mark on and off the field. Now Mark tries to be loving and supportive of his children too.

Ever since he became a dad, Mark has always made being a good father a high priority. He always takes time to attend his children's baseball games, dance recitals, and karate competitions. He also loves to just hang out with the children and play. He says that being a dad is one of the greatest gifts that God has given him. His children will tell you that they have the greatest daddy in the whole world. Guess that's why he's an all-pro dad!

A Soccer Coach's Bigger Goal

Alex Ferguson of Manchester United is one of the most successful soccer coaches in the world. As Ferguson was recently preparing for a big play-off match, his son approached him in the team's hotel lobby and said,

"Dad, I want you to know that no matter what happens today, you're a great father and a great soccer coach. I'll love you no less twelve hours from now than I do right now. My love for you won't change based on what will or won't happen during the soccer game tonight."

Well, it was quite a game indeed. Manchester United was down 1 to 0 with only a couple of minutes remaining. The words of Ferguson's son echoed throughout his mind during the entire game. Needless to say, the team scored two goals in the final two minutes to cap one of the most incredible soccer matches in recent history. Ferguson is a tremendous coach, but even more important, he's attained a more valuable goal—being a good father.

A Man of Honor

We've all been impressed by the courage and honor displayed by our servicemen and servicewomen. A very inspiring story surrounds a soldier in the Civil War named James Tanner. James was a schoolteacher, but when the Civil War started, he enlisted as fast as he could. He served as a corporal at the Battle of Second Bull Run and received wounds that required the amputation of both legs. Did James wallow in self-pity? No. He learned how to walk with artificial legs. But here's the real inspiration—on the evening of April 14, 1865—he was by the side of the dying Abraham Lincoln and took comprehensive notes of the entire assassination to help his government. He later founded a veteran's organization to help soldiers in distress. He overcame adversity to end up serving his president and country in ways he could never possibly imagine.

The Rare Jewel of Loyalty

Charles Colson, who served under Richard Nixon and went to prison for the Watergate scandal, relates a very interesting story. Shortly after he got out of jail, Colson gave a speech at a very prestigious university. While trying to speak, he was constantly interrupted by hecklers. At one point, a student stood up and yelled,

"Hey, Colson—why did you cover for Nixon?"

Charles put aside his papers, looked at the student, and said, "Because he was my friend."

The audience then spontaneously burst into applause. Colson later mused about why the crowd clapped. The best reason he could come up with is that there is so very little true loyalty today. Certainly there are very few that would go to prison for a friend. And while Colson was wrong in his involvement with Watergate, there is something admirable about a man willing to take the fall for someone else.

We Could Learn from a Man in a Kilt

"Men don't follow titles—they follow courage," said Scottish hero William Wallace in the movie *Braveheart*. The same goes for fathering. Kids don't follow a man just because he has the title of their father. They follow him because he has the courage to love them, to provide for them, and to sacrifice for them. You have to earn respect from your kids every day—and they will follow you. Best of all, you can do all this in just a regular pair of khakis.

Are You a Winner or a Whiner?

Two different people. Two similar circumstances. Yet one will emerge a winner, the other a whiner. The difference? Their attitude. Consider what Charles Swindoll says in his book Strengthening Your Grip,

> Words can never adequately convey the incredible impact of our attitude toward life. The longer I live the more convinced I become that life is 10 percent what happens to us and 90 percent how we respond to it.
>
> I believe the single most significant decision I can make on a day-to-day basis is my choice of attitude. It is more important than my past, my education, my bankroll, my successes or failures, fame or pain, what other people think of me or say about me, my circumstances, or my position. Attitude keeps me going or cripples my progress. It alone fuels my fire or assaults my hope. When my attitudes are right, there's no barrier too high, no valley too deep, no dream too extreme, no challenge too great for me.
>
> —*Strengthening Your Grip,* by Charles R. Swindoll (Nashville, Tenn.: W. Publishing Group, 1982), pp. 206–7. Used by permission of Insight for Living, Plano, TX 75026

Are You a Parent Who Is Troubled over a Broken Relationship with Your Child?

Ernest Hemingway wrote about a Spanish father and son whose relationship was shattered. When the rebellious son ran away, the father placed an ad in the newspaper saying,

"Paco, please meet me in front of the newspaper office at noon. All is forgiven. Love, Father." He was amazed the next day when 800 sons, all named Paco, showed up seeking reconciliation with their fathers. If you're facing a strained relationship with one of your kids, maybe today is the day for you to reach out to him or her with love and forgiveness. For 364 other great tidbits pick up the book, *Family Minutes,* by visiting http://www.allprodad.com/generalfatherestore.asp.

Today's Fathering Tip Comes from Alexander the Great

While Alexander the Great was out in the battlefield conquering the known world, one of his young troops in the heat of battle had a sudden attack of cowardice, turned, and ran away from the fighting. Later, his fellow soldiers tracked him down and brought him to Alexander's tent. Alexander looked at him and said,

"Son, what is your name?"

To which he replied, "It's Alexander."

Then Alexander responded: "Well, then either change your actions or change your name!" Your children carry the reputation of your name with them. Be a man of honor so they can have a name to live up to.

You Didn't Get a Divorce from Your Kids

No words exist to adequately describe what a father goes through when he gets divorced. He loses a wife with whom he intended to spend the rest of his life. He often loses his legacy by being removed from his own children. But does he have to lose his legacy? No.

Many dads simply give up and walk away from their biological children because they believe that everything is now pointless. They feel that because they won't be around much, it doesn't really matter. Other fathers do the "every other weekend" thing. They'll have the kids over to just hang out and have some fun without being involved in the rest of their lives.

But there is another option—do your best to remain cordial with your ex and don't talk about her negatively to your kids. This way you'll gain greater access to your children. You may be able to call many evenings and read them a bedtime story over the phone. You can go to parent-teacher conferences. You can send them a variety of greeting cards and bring them souvenirs from business trips. You can attend their sporting events and music recitals. Whatever it is, your children need you involved. You didn't get a divorce from them. You're their father. Forever.

How Does a Stepparent Discipline?

How does a stepparent discipline? The answer—very carefully. Experts say that in the beginning of a stepparenting relationship, the disciplining should be left to the biological parent. The stepparent can still be involved in deciding on rules and consequences, but the biological parent should do the actual enforcing. Meanwhile, the stepparent can show affection, share values, and set limits. So concentrate on laying a good foundation until your relationship develops and the time is right for you to share in the disciplining.

If You're Divorced, Are You Using Your Children for Revenge?

Divorce is not easy. It's often accompanied by a lot of bitterness and disappointment, and many people want to get back at their former spouses. Unfortunately, they use their children to do it, doing things like not letting their ex spend additional time with the kids, even if it's in the children's best interest. Or they put the child in the middle, using them to get information about their former spouse. Think about how unfair and damaging that is. Instead, put your child's needs before your own, and leave revenge out of the picture.

Dads at a Distance

Divorced? Live far away from your kids? If so, here are some ways to help you stay connected. First, be involved in their education. Give your child's teachers pre-addressed, stamped envelopes so they can send you updates. Make sure you see report cards and test grades. Also, e-mail or call as often as you can. For younger children, personally record reading a bedtime story. Make a video of yourself, your office, and your pets. Send these tapes on a regular basis so your children can see you, hear you, and know how much you love them. For more information contact *Dads at a Distance* at www.daads.com

Saving Your Second Marriage

If you've gone through the pain of divorce and feel betrayed by your ex, your vision and expectations for a possible second marriage might be clouded. In fact, 60 percent of second marriages fail. If you're thinking about getting married again, you need to consider factors such as whether you're really ready, whether you really know your potential mate, and whether you'll be able to avoid the same mistakes that caused your first divorce. Seek counseling from a church or counselor to help you properly weigh these enormous issues.

Being Sensitive to Single Moms

Are some of your coworkers single mothers? Have you stopped to think how much of their lives they spend doing things for others? They usually have to get up early, feed and dress the kids, send them off to school, then work a full day and come home to feed and nurture their children, as well as deal with headaches such as bills and leaky pipes. It's been said that if you want to know how much the world weighs, just ask a single mother.

So, plan to go out of your way to help a single mom whenever you can. She has an awfully tough job—both inside and outside the workplace.

Even If You're Not Living with Your Children, You Still Matter Tremendously to Them

In a study entitled "Nonresident Fathers and Children's Well-Being," it was found that "the child feeling close to the non-resident father . . . positively and significantly correlated with higher academic achievement and fewer behavioral and emotional problems for both boys and girls."

Make no mistake about it—you still have a crucial role in helping to raise your children even if you can't see them every day.

NFL Fans Can Be Fickle

When their favorite team starts to accumulate more losses than wins, fans can come up with some pretty creative names to show their displeasure. For example: Kansas City Griefs, Oakland Faders, Indianapolis Dolts, and the Green Bay Slackers, to name only a few. And while NFL players may not appreciate being labeled "faders," they understand it's part of the game.

However, children take name-calling much more seriously. And while many kids struggle with being taunted at school or on the playground, some kids also have to endure being called names like "dummy" and "idiot" at home by their parents. That can set your children up for some serious problems. They'll begin to form a self-image based on these put-downs and will live up to those names. So make sure you speak positively to your children. And if you just can't resist, save those put-downs for the teams on your television screen.

Do Your Children Have an
Attitude of Gratitude?

Raising a grateful child has never been more challenging. Our kids are constantly bombarded by ads from businesses that try persuading them that they should have their every wish fulfilled. The message is that they need more—so their parents need to buy more. And even if they do get everything they want, they take it for granted. A grateful person is shaped to appreciate, not just acquire. Take every opportunity to show your kids what appreciation looks like—thank Mom for a good meal, thank the mail carrier for faithfully delivering the mail, and thank the Little League coach for giving his or her time. An attitude of gratitude—it's a gift they'll learn to appreciate.

Listen to What Your
Kids Are Listening To

Having trouble deciphering exactly what it is your kids are listening to? In between the clang of guitars and drums, a message is being sent. And while it might be hard for you to pick up what the singer is singing (or screaming), you're probably more than a little concerned about what kind of message your kids are getting. So there's an easy solution—ask to see the lyrics that came with the CD or tape. If the album didn't come with lyrics or the lyrics were conveniently "lost," most bands have their own web sites where you can usually read the lyrics for yourself.

So, dads, make a concerted effort to tune in to what your kids are listening to. For information on great-sounding bands with wholesome lyrics, go to http://www.familyfirst. net/musicchart.asp.

Here's a Lesson from a Losing Record

A sport's team general manager commented on his team's 7-27 record by saying, "We can't win at home. We can't win on the road. As general manager, I just can't figure out where else to play." While this is certainly an amusing insight into sports, it also can be a commentary on fatherhood. You see, many dads feel guilty for spending too much time at the office, yet when they arrive home, they feel they're not very successful there either. But the keys to success, whether in sports or as a dad, are planning and perseverance.

Plan on spending quality time with your kids doing things they like to do—not just having them tag along while you run errands. And persevere with your children. Continue to love and converse with them even when your patience is thin and it seems as though you're not getting through. You are. And as opposed to football, where winning isn't everything, in fatherhood it *is* everything.

Budget a Better Family

One of the biggest stress creators in family life is money. Not having enough financial strength can cause unlimited problems and strains on relationships. Surprisingly, a chief cause of financial problems is not lack of money but the unwise spending of it. And one of the best ways to solve this problem is to have a budget, by which money is allocated for food, clothing, savings, and so on. So dads, if you haven't done so already, put together a simple spreadsheet so you can track expenses. And encourage your children to budget as well. Sure, you may have to cut back a bit in some areas, but the gain will be invaluable—a better quality of family life.

Yes, Girls Can Play Sports Too!

Sometimes the fathers of girls think ballet and piano lessons are the only way to go when raising young ladies. But that's not necessarily the case. As a matter of fact, girls need to learn about good sportsmanship just as much as boys do. And high school girls who play sports are less likely to get pregnant or take drugs and are more likely to graduate. So don't rule out sports for girls—it may be yet another great way for you to bond with your daughter.

Does Your Correcting Need Correction?

Many times when a dad disciplines, the results can actually be worse than if he never disciplined at all. If your kids feel less loved or less important after being corrected, you're sowing seeds of harm in them in the long run. Instead, realize that there's *always* a positive way to speak to children, even when you need to correct them. Point out what needs to be changed, but also state how much you love them. Then impress upon them that you know they'll behave better because you believe in them.

Child Abductions

Child abduction is a growing problem in our society; therefore, parents of small children need to take proper precautions. In a recent article in *Parents* magazine, Herman Gray, chief of staff of Children's Hospital of Michigan, said that parents should begin teaching their children about strangers as soon as they can clearly understand who strangers are.

"Three to four years of age is probably the earliest this can begin for most children. . . . Teaching your child not to go anywhere with a stranger or not to take anything from a stranger is better than to discuss abductions, which might be too frightening for your young children." Dr. Gray advises parents to make sure to speak simply. For example, "A stranger is someone not in our family like Mommy or Daddy or Susie or Grandma."

We live, unfortunately, in dangerous times. Make sure your children stay safe.

Talk to Your Kids about
Appropriate Adult Behavior

Unfortunately, we live in a society where small minorities of adults prey on children. Make sure you teach your kids how adults should behave toward them, including appropriate and inappropriate touching and conversation. Also make sure your kids can come to you if they think they've been exploited in some way. Sometimes children feel shame or embarrassment regarding such incidents and initially do not want to tell their parents.

So drive home the point that you'll always care for them and do what it takes to protect them. That's your most important job as a father.

Tying Toddlers into Your Day

If you're the parent of a toddler, you may realize that he or she loves to imitate you and your daily tasks. Doing chores is a great example. So instead of getting frustrated when your toddler gets in your way, provide him or her ways to "help" you. For instance, if you're dusting, give your toddler his or her own little dust rag. Or provide a toy lawnmower to use while you're mowing. This will prove to be a great way for you to interact with your toddler. Your child will feel appreciated and needed, and it will teach him or her the importance of pitching in and helping the family.

Have You and Your Wife Experienced the Pain of a Miscarriage?

According to the National Center for Fathering, nearly 10 percent of women with no history of miscarriages will lose a child. And percentages indicate that those who have had one miscarriage have a greater potential for even another miscarriage. While the hurt runs very deep, there are some steps you can take to help with the pain.

- If you're able to do it, tell your children about the loss of your child.
- Check with a father who has experienced the loss of a child this past year. Ask him specifically how he's holding up and dealing with the situation. Be available to listen if he wants to talk more about his grief.
- And most importantly, talk to your wife about the grieving process. Discuss how each of you are grieving during this time of loss. Seek to understand her feelings and commit to the healing process together.

For a free info sheet on miscarriage, go to http://www.allprodad.com/2miscarriage.asp.

© 2003 by The National Center for Fathering

Relishing Repetition

If there's one constant about raising small children, it's seeing how much they enjoy repetition. A small boy will climb up and go down a slide for hours on end and be perfectly content. A young girl will enjoy jumping rope for quite an extended amount of time in your driveway. You see, for a child, there's an incredible capacity for wonder in doing what adults see as trivial. There's quite a temptation for dads to think they always have to entertain the kids or plop them in front of the newest movie. But don't underestimate the simple things in life that can bring them so much joy. It's the capacity of wonder and the contentment in simple things that make a child's life so wonderful.

New Fathers Shouldn't Be Intimidated

If you're a new father, you may be a bit unsure of how to handle this new bundle of joy. Do you just let your wife take care of the baby while you offer standoffish advice? Or do you bravely hold the child and even tackle diaper changing? It's important for you to interact with your new baby. Specifically, infants with involved fathers smile more frequently and explore their surroundings more. By six weeks of age, infants can distinguish their father's voice from their mother's voice. A classic study from Boston Children's Hospital found that infants anticipate different interaction from their fathers than their mothers.

So dads, roll up your sleeves, grab the bib and talcum powder, and experience the joy!

There Are All Kinds of Different Thoughts about Discipline Out There

Viewpoints on discipline vary widely. There's the heavy-handed view of just "give your kids a good whippin'." Then there's the hands-off, "just let them express themselves without consequences," approach. So how is a father to decide how to correct his children when there are experts on both sides of the discipline issue? The National Center for Fathering has some guidelines:

- Discuss with your wife the specifics of discipline
- Give your children well-defined guidelines
- Be consistent in correction when your children step outside the guidelines
- Model self-discipline yourself.

© 2004 by The National Center for Fathering

These four principles will help you set a foundation for effective and fair discipline for your children.

"Working as a coach in the NFL has been incredibly exciting, challenging, and demanding, but it doesn't compare to the responsibility, effort, and fulfillment of trying to be a top flight dad. I've had the opportunity to work with world-class athletes at the top of their profession and see the hard work and effort it takes. ALL-PRO DAD can help fathers experience the joy of making it to the top of their premier job—a father!"

Clyde Christensen

—Clyde Christensen, Assistant Coach
2002–2003—Indianapolis Colts;
1996–2001—Tampa Bay Buccaneers

Clyde Christensen is a native of California. He was born in the town of Covina in 1958 to an unwed teenage mother. She gave him up for adoption, and he found his way into the home and hearts of Dick and June Christensen. Clyde says, "All the good things I learned came from them."

Clyde says the word that describes his father is "available." He says his dad was always there when he needed him. In the area of athletics, he not only attended all of Clyde's sporting events but also all his practices. Even now, not a week goes by without Clyde's dad calling him to express his love and affirmation.

That is also the kind of father Clyde strives to be with his own family. He and his wife, Debbie, have three daughters—Rachel, Rebecca, and Ruth. Clyde stays involved in his daughters' lives and is committed to a close relationship with each of them. He admits that balancing coaching and fatherhood can be challenging but stresses that he and all other dads need to make being a good father a priority. He says the rewards of doing so will be seen throughout this lifetime and in the generations to come.

Teens and Sexuality

A recent feature story in *U.S. News and World Report* focused on teens and sexuality. The report finds that kids from all walks of life are having sex at younger and younger ages. Nearly one in ten youth reports losing his or her virginity before the age of thirteen. This is a 15 percent increase since 1997 according to the Centers for Disease Control and Prevention. Some 16 percent of high school sophomores have had four or more sexual partners. Two-thirds of high school seniors report they have engaged in intercourse. And tragically, while teenage sex is on the rise, only 48 percent of the parents of teens even bring up the subject, and only 11 percent of parents bring it up regularly. What a tragedy! Be part of that 11 percent, or your kids might very well end up being another unfortunate statistic.

Smoking at the Movies

We've already mentioned the importance of talking to your kids about smoking, and if you don't, Hollywood will. Case in point: screenwriter, Joe Eszterhas, who put many smoking scenes into popular movies, wrote in the *New York Times* that "a cigarette in the hands of a Hollywood star on-screen is a gun aimed at a 12- or 14-year-old." Ironically, Joe now also suffers from throat cancer, and this apparently has awakened him to the dangers cigarettes pose. So tackle the subject of smoking with your kids before it's too late.

Are Your Children Dressing Inappropriately?

It's a constant battle for most parents—our society condones and promotes improper attire. Just check out all of the scantily clad people displayed on magazine covers at your local grocery store checkout stand. But your kids should be called to a different standard. There's a proper philosophy in dressing modestly. This philosophy desires to put the emphasis where it should be—on a person's personality, not on his or her anatomical makeup.

So stand fast with your kids. Let them know that their most important characteristics are those that can't be seen, thus, you'll not allow them to look superficial and wear clothing that allows too much to be seen.

Are Your Kids Giving You a Hard Time about Your "Old-Fashioned" Rules?

Maybe you won't let your kids go out on a single date until a certain age or have told them they may not buy that halter top. If you're like most dads, you'll get the infamous, "But why?" Try to use that opportunity to discuss the situation rather than just answer, "Well, just because."

G. K. Chesterton said, "Before you pull any fence down, always pause long enough to find out why it was put there in the first place."

Ask your children why they think you put that fence of rules in place. In the end, though they still might not like being restricted, they'll know you care enough about them to want to protect them.

Teens and Sexuality 2

According to *U.S. News and World Report,* parents can make a difference when it comes to their teenagers' sexual behavior. In a study published in 2000, the National Teen Pregnancy Prevention Research Center analyzed interviews with 3,322 virginal eighth to eleventh graders and their moms. Some of these teens had mothers who didn't disapprove of their having sex. Others knew their moms disapproved of their having sex at the time. At a follow-up interview that occurred after nine to eighteen months, kids in the latter group were far more likely to be virgins. Imagine that! Some teenagers still listen to their parents—even when the subject is sex.

What Happens When a Young Man Tells You He Loves Your Daughter?

The author C. S. Lewis broke down love into two categories: "gift-love" and "need-love." He uses the following example in his book *The Four Loves:* "Need-love says of a woman 'I cannot live without her' and is self-centered; gift-love longs to give her happiness, comfort and protection. . . . Gift-love would be that love which moves a man to work and plan and save for the future well-being of his children's family which he will die without sharing or seeing."

You see, true love longs to give, not take. A man who wishes to date your daughter should understand the difference—and so should you.

God Willing, Your Kids Will Never Be Suicidal

But we all need to be aware of certain warning signs to look for. You or your kids will most likely come across teens who are seriously contemplating suicide. If you fear that someone may take his or her life, get help immediately. Call a government agency, church, counseling service, or similar organization. Here are some crucial characteristics to be on the lookout for in possibly suicidal teens:

- If they say things like "I don't want to live anymore" or "I hate myself," pay attention.
- If they're constantly depressed, have substance abuse problems, withdraw, show less interest in usual interests, and live in a school or work environment that encourages depression.

These teens are at risk for suicide. About 80 percent of those who attempt suicide do exhibit signs. Be aware of suicidal tendencies. Suicide is a dark reality for many teens today.

Are Your Kids Mystified by Their Report Card?

Have you ever heard your kid say, "Dad, I don't know how in the world I got a D. I thought I was doing really well."

If this or a similar statement is typically spoken by your kids, here's a great idea—have them keep track of all their tests, homework, and report grades. Either on paper or on the computer, tell your kids to record their grades every time they get graded, and then they (and you) can keep a constant watch on their academic status. If you have a computer, create a spreadsheet that constantly averages their scores so they know where they stand and what they need to do to get the best grade they can. For a free article on other homework hints visit http://www.allprodad.com/6homeworkhints.asp.

Tired of the Garbage Coming over Some Television Channels?

If you're disturbed by what's making it onto television these days, you can do something about it and protect your family.

- First, you can call your cable or satellite company to complain, and they might be able to give you some helpful suggestions.
- You can also buy a "lockbox" either from them or at a retail store. The "lockbox" is designed to block offensive channels that concern you.
- Also, there's now a new device on the market called a "V" chip. All newer televisions have this chip which can be used to identify and block shows you and your family find offensive.

Take control of your television, or it will take control of your kids.

Introducing Your Parents to Your Great-Grandchildren

Videotaping an interview with your parents will be a true treasure for future generations. Your children's children and their children will be able to see their great-grandparents and get a taste of what it was like to grow up in the twentieth century. ALL-PRO DAD has put together a free information sheet of great interview questions to ask your parents. Visit http://www.allprodad.com/9familymemories.asp and make memories that will last well over a hundred years!

Are Your Kids Craving Expensive Name-Brand Clothes?

Do your kids seem stuck on name-brand clothes? Do they seem oblivious to how much they cost? Then here's a compromise if you're purchasing their apparel. Agree to pay what you believe is a fair price for their new clothes or shoes. If they want the more expensive brands, then they'll have to pay the difference out of their own pocket. All of a sudden, the logo on the outside of the shirt or the name of the shoe may become decidedly less important to them. Or they may really want the name brand and will take better care of the products now that they have a stake in them. Either way, you both win.

Saying "Sir" Isn't a Slur

Do your kids speak respectfully to you and other grown-ups? I know it sounds old-fashioned, but I'm a big fan of kids saying, "Yes, sir" to men and "Yes, ma'am" to women. Adults are floored when they hear children use those terms and are always impressed and pleased. When a child speaks to adults respectfully, it instills in the kids honor and decorum—two characteristics that will pay huge dividends down the road. So if you haven't already, get your kids into this habit. And a great place to start is right in your home.

How Often Do Your Kids Touch Base with Their Grandparents?

Do your kids have regular contact with their grandparents, or is it only on birthdays and holidays? As your parents age and begin to think about how they've spent their lives, one of the most important things to them is to know that their family—and especially their grandkids—love them and care about them. So make it a practice to frequently call, visit, and write your folks and your wife's folks. And develop this routine so that it's visible to your children. You want your children to develop this same pattern of keeping in continued contact with their grandparents.

Want to Broaden Your Kids' Horizons?

If you have younger children that cannot quite grasp the content of *Newsweek* or *U.S. News and World Report,* then think about getting them a subscription to a quality children's magazine, such as, *National Geographic Kids Magazine* or *Time Kids Magazine.* Both of these magazines are great choices to get your kids involved in exploring the world around them without leaving the living room. Talk to your children about their interests, and then do a little exploring on the Internet to find out which kids' magazines would best match your kids' interests. Get them interested and you'll get them reading.

The Swimsuit Issue Is an Issue

A lot of husbands will thumb through a *Sports Illustrated* swimsuit issue or a mail-order lingerie catalog and then make offhand comments about how attractive the featured women are. This can be emotionally disturbing to your wife, even if she doesn't say much about it. Most women feel a lot of pressure to conform to a body image that's completely unrealistic. It's no secret that many models have eating disorders just to be what pop culture calls attractive. So stuff your insensitive comments. Better yet, stuff those periodicals into your trash can. Want to really get on your wife's good side? Then send her a free ALL-PRO DAD e-card by visiting http://www.allprodad.com/compose.html.

The Key to Discipline
Is Parental Unity

Parents who are not on the same wavelength when it comes to discipline will have a whole host of problems. Children will try to play one parent against another in order to get out of trouble. This is especially true when one parent is significantly "softer" than the other. So talk with your wife and make sure you're unified when it comes to discipline. Don't undermine each other. You'll find discipline a whole lot more effective when both you and your spouse are consistent.

Does Your Wife Have a Little
Time to Herself in the Evening?

Whether your wife spent her day at the office or spent her day dealing with the children, chances are she's tired and could use a little time to relax. It's amazing how a brief window of rest can rejuvenate the soul. So offer to watch the kids for a bit while she lies down, reads, talks with some friends, goes shopping, or whatever. With all she does for you and your family, it's one way to give back just a little.

Honesty Is the Best Policy

Are you holding on to a grudge for something your wife did sometime ago? Do you even realize that she may have no idea that she even offended you? It's commonly said there are really three views in every circumstance—what you perceived, what the other person perceived, and what actually happened. You see, your wife may have a completely different outlook on that same situation, which is why it pays to be honest with her about your feelings. Seeing her point of view may alleviate some of your stress, while having her recognize your views will help her to be more sensitive in that area in the future.

A Marriage Constant: Change

An old proverb states:

> A woman enters a marriage expecting to change a man. She can't.
> A man enters a marriage expecting the woman to stay the same. She won't.

And, men, it's true. Your wife is constantly evolving physically, mentally, emotionally, and spiritually. You have to keep up with the changes. And change isn't necessarily bad—sometimes it's for the better. But you need to adapt as she changes. A man is successful in marriage when he's constantly attuned to his wife's needs and is striving to meet those needs.

How Much Do You Know about PDAs?

PDAs—how much do you know about them? No, not the handheld devices you try to figure out while driving and accidentally back up through a store window while getting a phone number. How much do you know about *public displays of affection*? Do you have any idea how much your wife loves it when you put your arm around her while at the store or hold her hand during church? How often do you consistently do this? And if you did it when you were first dating, why has it gone by the wayside?

Make your wife's day—show some PDA.

I Take Myself to Have and to Hold . . .

According to *World* magazine, Jennifer Hoes is planning the first postmodern marriage. She'll be both bride and groom at her wedding in the Netherlands.

"We live in a 'me' society," she says. "Hence, it is logical that one promises to be faithful to oneself."

Jennifer plans a $22,000 reception for her relatives. One wonders what would happen if she ever wanted to get a divorce. Jennifer's outlook is both ridiculous and sad. But how many people get married out of their own selfish desires and needs rather than to give to the other person? Marriage is about self-sacrifice. And as the man, this starts with you.

Snap, Crackle, Drop?

A current NFL player said he had just one uniform in college, and he had to personally wash it after each practice. He was the sixteenth choice of the 1985 pro football draft. When he was a rookie, he was continually dropping passes. One newspaper headline focusing on this rookie read, "Snap, Crackle, Drop." After overcoming such obstacles, Jerry Rice soon dominated the NFL game and is considered the greatest wide receiver of all time. But he's also a family man. According to columnist Larry Schwartz, Jerry's wife (Jackie) said that Jerry sometimes comes home from a game and cleans the house. From scoring touchdowns to scrubbing toilets, Jerry plays to win.

Coach Dungy

Too busy to spend time with your kids? If you answered yes, an NFL head coach wants a few words with you. Tony Dungy of the Indianapolis Colts has a demanding schedule, but he still makes family the biggest part of his game plan. He takes time to be with his children, picking them up from school and bringing them to the office. He says fatherhood, not football, is his most important job.

So take a look at your game plan. Strategize time with your kids. Maybe it's taking them to school; maybe it's fixing them breakfast. The point is—if an NFL head coach can make time to be a good dad, you can too.

Man of Steel and Velvet

Poet Carl Sandburg described Abraham Lincoln as a man of steel and velvet. He was referring to Lincoln's unique combination of strong qualities of integrity, honesty, and courage, and his softer qualities of compassion, friendliness, and love for others. To be a man of steel and velvet, like Abraham Lincoln, a man cannot place too much emphasis on either his steel side or his velvet side. It's having a perfect balance of strength and compassion that can make a man a better husband and father—a man of steel and velvet.

Parenting Advice from Winston Churchill

On October 29, 1941, Britain had been at war with Germany for over two years. It was a dark time for this proud nation. On that day Winston Churchill delivered his famous speech, saying, "Never give in. Never give in. Never, never, never." This may be your darkest hour as a dad. You just caught your child with drugs. Your teenage daughter just told you she's pregnant. Your son is sitting in jail. Well, now is *not* the time to surrender. Continue to fight for your child. Never give in. Never give up. Never, never, never.

What Is the Essence of Love?

When you love someone, what does it really mean? Spending time with him or her? Giving the person gifts? Complimenting him or her? These can all be good things. But true love is all about self-sacrifice. It's about taking your wife on a weekend antiquing trip when you would rather be watching a football game. It's about listening to your little daughter talk nonstop about everything she created out of Play-Doh® that morning. Love seeks only to give, never to get. Yet, in a spectacular way, you reap love back when you sow it abundantly.

Daunte Culpepper

Eighty-four-year-old Emma Culpepper has adopted fourteen children over her lifetime. Twenty years ago she adopted a one-day-old boy who had been born in prison. Emma raised him with love and discipline. He went on to set football records at the University of Central Florida and is one of the premier quarterbacks in the NFL today. Daunte Culpepper is living out his dream because of the sacrifice and love of a woman named Emma. She had the compassion and heart to give a little baby born in prison a future full of hope.

Peer Pressure Doesn't Affect Kids Only

Let's talk about the peer pressure you face, you know—the push from society to have the big house, nice car, and all the trimmings. While these things aren't necessarily bad in and of themselves, what it takes to get them might be. If you're sacrificing your family relationships for material goods, you're missing out.

So don't be so concerned with keeping up with the Joneses, because while you may have a lot of money—if you neglect your family, you'll never be truly rich.

"Two of the single most defining moments in my life were the birth of my two children. But the responsibility is huge. ALL-PRO DAD gives me and other men the necessary equipment we need to have a positive impact on our children and the people they interact with."

—Todd Peterson, Kicker 2003—San Francisco 49ers; 2002—Pittsburgh Steelers; 2000–2001— Kansas City Chiefs; 1995–1999— Seattle Seahawks; 1994—Arizona Cardinals

The life of a military family is not exactly easy. Todd Peterson knows this firsthand. He was born February 4, 1970, in Washington, D.C., to Greg (a United States Air Force base commander) and Jouree Peterson. Living all over the country and overseas meant moving away from friends and trying to make new ones. Fortunately, for Todd and his younger sister, Clair, their military father showed continuous love, guidance, and support that made their changing lifestyle all the more bearable.

Add to the stress of moving the fact that Todd was a standout athlete, and you have one confused and stressed-out kid. The pressure from parents to excel and sometimes overachieve can be difficult for a young athlete. This, however, was not something that Todd ever experienced. Greg Peterson gave his children unconditional love and encouragement. He taught them to work hard and be honest but never to let their identity get tied up in performance. This is precisely how Todd has begun raising his two young children, Hannah and Zach. Todd feels that being a parent is a huge responsibility but an even greater privilege. He stands by the Bible's teaching that children are a gift from the Lord.

Todd and his wife, Susan, are committed to raising their children in a loving Christian home. Both are very active in Young Life, a Christian youth organization, for which Susan worked from 1994 to 1998. Todd tries to instill the same good Christian values in Hannah and Zach that he promotes through his work in the community. He understands that he has an impact on everyone with whom his children come in contact. Todd believes that this is the biggest issue with fathers today, and he hopes to reach out to those fathers by being an all-pro dad.

All-Pro Dads Are Worldwide

Good fathers come in all shapes and sizes, but they have one thing in common—an unparalleled love for their kids. And sometimes the best way for dads to help their kids is for dads to help each other. That's why we're proud to announce an international component to our ALL-PRO DAD program. Visit us at http://www.allprodad.com/community.asp to see the countries we have contacts in. Our goal is to try to foster communication no matter where dads might live in the world. If you don't see your country, let us know. While the world might have grown smaller in the last century, parenting issues are just as big.

So use this opportunity to communicate to fathers who are just across the street—or across the world. Meet dads from all over the world by visiting http://www.allprodad.com/community.asp.

It All Starts with the First Five Minutes

The first five minutes of the day between a dad and his children sets the tone for the entire work day and for that school day. Harsh words or tension as the kids gather for breakfast will turn the relationship sunny-side down. But greeting your children in the morning with hugs and kisses is a great way to kick off a day. And at the end of the day, tucking your kids into bed with words of praise will once again set the tone for tomorrow.

Raising Good Kids Doesn't Mean Raising Your Voice

Sometimes when dealing with your children, you may have a tendency to emphasize an important point by raising your voice, rather than reinforcing your authority. There are times when you didn't really mean to yell, but it just comes out that way. And it's not good for your kids to hear you speak like that. So go back and apologize if you need to. But also take that opportunity to explain to them why you were so upset. Your children are much more likely to listen and obey your wishes in the future when you talk calmly.

So, dads, remember—it's not only what you say but how you say it.

All Baseball Players Are Failures

Warren Spahn, the winningest left-hander in baseball history said, as he addressed a group of senators:

> Baseball is a game of failure. Even the best batters fail about 65 percent of the time. Hall of Fame pitchers lose more games than a team plays in a full season. I just hope you fellows in Congress have more success than baseball players have.

Successful baseball players deal with failure constantly but are able to overcome it. It's no different than successful fathers. We can and do fail—but it's important to realize that failure is a part of raising children. And it's learning and growing from these shortcomings that in the end will help us be better dads.

Are Your Kids Constantly Saying Unkind Things to Each Other?

Are you tired of continually telling your kids to stop saying unkind things to each other? Well, do more than that. Each time your kids begin to throw verbal darts at each other—take action. Immediately begin to revoke some of their privileges. This lets your kids know that you mean business and will immediately begin to curb some of their fighting, at least in front of you. Secondly, set the example. Make sure you're not talking down to either your wife or kids. Make your household one that speaks words of encouragement to each other—and not harm. You'll find your family a much happier one. And, as hymn writer John Bowring comments, "A happy family is but an earlier heaven."

Accountability—It's a Good Thing

Accountability! It's a word that's been used quite a bit lately as some major corporations have been accused of fudging numbers to pad their bottom lines. Even though accountability is crucial in the business world, it's also vital in family life. Fathers should be accountable not only to their wives and kids but also to a couple of close male friends. It's a great idea to set aside a little time during the week—say an early-morning breakfast—to meet with a couple of other like-minded guys and discuss topics like faith, family, job stress, and life goals. Good friends can offer you much-needed encouragement and perspective.

So seriously consider making yourself accountable. It is a return on an investment you'll never regret.

Do You Have a Tendency to Be Overcritical of Your Children's Athletic Abilities?

Let's face it, dads, we can be way too competitive. It takes only a trip down to the local Little League fields to hear men yelling out unnecessary comments to their kids (and other fans). There is always the temptation for us to lecture our children on how to shoot a better free throw or toss a curveball that will nick the corner of the plate. But too much of this sermonizing, and sports will become a drudgery to our children—not a joy. The result: Our children will play, not because they like the sport, but because they want to please us. And that's not what an all-pro dad should want.

Put 'em to Work

I f you have children who are able to do chores but not quite able to head out into the workforce, here are a few ideas to keep them busy and learn the value of a dollar:

- Make a list of the things that need to be done around the house, above and beyond their normal duties, and have them sign up to do them. Make it clear as to how much they'll earn for each job so you won't have an unpleasant situation at the end.
- Call a church, nursing home, or other organization to see if there are odd jobs your kids can do for them or the people they care for. The organization might be able to reimburse your kids a little, or you could reward your kids yourself.
- Have your kids talk to neighbors to see if they can do any garage cleaning, yard work, or other jobs for them. It's surprising how much work can be found right in your own neighborhood.

Your kids will grow in character as a result of working. Give them the privilege of doing so.

Choosing Your Own
Family Adventure

Here's a creative idea—put together a family storybook. Here's how it works. One family member begins by writing a one-page piece with a cliff-hanger ending. The second family member picks up from there and writes another page with an added cliff-hanger ending. Do this until all the family members have contributed. Then read the story together and watch the tears of laughter roll. It'll weave a tale you can't forget!

Do You Have a Cap on How
Much Time Your Children
Spend Watching Television?

If you don't have a limit on your children's television-viewing time, it would be a good idea to institute it. Otherwise, they'll always want to watch television from dawn to dusk and will pout if you want them to shut off the tube early. You can give your kids their daily or weekly television time quota and let them decide how to spend it. You could also create a pool of time in which misbehavior causes them to lose their "television time." Let your children know that TV time is a privilege, not a right. And life is bigger than a thirty-two-inch screen.

If Your Kids Could Change One Thing

Here's a scary question to ask your kids that could really help make your relationship with them much stronger:
IF YOU COULD CHANGE ONE THING ABOUT ME, WHAT WOULD IT BE?

Tell them they won't get in trouble, and you won't get mad. You just want to know how you can show them even more love. If they answer by saying that you lose your temper too much or you aren't around enough, make mental notes (or even actual notes) and reevaluate yourself. Ask your wife for input. See if there's an area where a little improvement will actually make a big improvement in your relationships with your kids.

Have You Checked Out Your Child's Booster Club?

Many schools have booster groups for athletic activities, cheerleading, music groups, and academic clubs. Why not get involved? This would be a great opportunity not only to help raise money for the things your children are doing but also it's a fantastic way to meet other parents. Forming friendships with other parents who have kids the same age as yours is a great thing to do. And booster activities are a ton of fun. So call your local school and get yourself signed up.

Caught Your Children Doing Something They Shouldn't?

Are your children at an age where they can read and write complete sentences? Rather then just giving them time-out for an offense, why not have them put together an essay on what they did wrong and how they'll abstain from it in the future? Writing a paper not only will force your kids to think about their indiscretion but will also enhance their literary skills as well. You may even ask them to do a little research to boot. Make sure the essay is done to the best of their ability. And let them know they're forgiven and loved. For a free article on how to have your kids write an essay, go to http://www.allprodad.com/6essaywriting.asp.

Do You Have a Family Mission Statement?

Most likely, your place of employment has a mission statement. What's the purpose of having one? It's to keep everyone on track with what the goals are and how you'll define success. And while it's great to know this in the corporate world, it's even better to know it for your family life. So put together a brief family mission statement and post it somewhere in your house. Every family's statement may be a little different, but here's an example:

THE GOAL OF OUR FAMILY IS TO CREATE A NURTURING AND LOVING ENVIRONMENT FOR EVERY MEMBER OF OUR FAMILY.

Then take the next step and talk to your family about how this goal (mission) will be accomplished. A great discussion is guaranteed!

Do Your Younger Children Suffer from "Snapshot Syndrome"?

The problem of "snapshot syndrome" is fairly common. Look over the photos you have of your kids. Do you notice that you took a lot more pictures of your firstborn as he or she was growing up—and that you don't have as many photos of your other children? When your first child was born, you were so excited that you were constantly taking pictures and video of him or her, literally, doing everything—the kinds of photos and videos that most other people would go into a near comatose state while viewing. But did some of that excitement wear off as you had more children? If so, be careful. Younger children, when they don't feel they're receiving the same amount of attention as older children, will try to get that attention in unpleasant ways. And that will certainly put you in an unpleasant mood.

So make a conscientious effort to give all your kids the same amount of attention. And keep that camcorder rolling.

Curbing Sibling Rivalry

If your wife is pregnant and you already have children, you may have to deal with some sibling rivalry. Here are a couple of helpful tips.

- Wrap up inexpensive gifts for the older child that can be given to him or her once the new baby is born. This will let the older child know that he or she is still appreciated and worth paying attention to.
- Also, if your older child starts behaving badly, talk to him or her about all the advantages of being older and bigger—and how he or she gets so many more privileges by virtue of age.

Make sure you show your child the attention needed. He or she will try to get it one way or another.

Boys and Books Can Be a Great Mix

After your son has learned to read, he needs to enjoy reading. Here are some ideas to motivate boys to read.

- Give him books on what he's interested in, like football or insects.
- Whenever you give your son a new toy, see if there's a book to go along with it. For instance, if you give him a toy plane, also give him a book on the history of flight.
- Set aside a special time each week for you and him to read together.

Books will open up a whole new world for him and can shape him into becoming a man of character. As Aristophanes said, "By words the mind is winged."

Selecting a Babysitter

Get recommendations from friends and family for a good babysitter. Ask the babysitter to come over before babysitting to make sure that he or she is comfortable with the house and interacts well with your children. Make the rules of the house clear and write down emergency phone numbers.

And don't be a cheapskate. Pay your babysitter well so he or she will be motivated to be flexible to your future needs.

Having Trouble with Some Picky Eaters?

It can be frustrating as a parent to prepare a meal for your kids only to see them scrunch up their noses at it. Arguments ensue, tempers flare, and the kids get sent to their room— you know the story. So here's a tip. Don't hit them with a full-fledged, brand-new meal. Instead prepare only a small portion of a new food that you want them to try. If they really can't stand it, don't punish them. Realize this is a learning test. They don't have to like everything you like. But if they start getting too finicky about everything prepared, then consequences should follow.

Is Your Child Afraid of the Boogeyman?

It may sound a bit ridiculous, but many small children are convinced that their room is haunted or that there's a monster under the bed. They'll have trouble falling asleep and may frequently call out to you in the middle of the night. Of course, having you come into their room while you're half asleep with your hair on end may not do anything to alleviate their fears, but talking to them in a calm voice, letting them know that you'll protect them, and encouraging them to think on good, safe things will go a long way in your epic battle against the boogeyman. And don't worry—your kids will outgrow their monster fears.

So in the meantime, just continue to tuck them in at night and give their room your "monster-free" seal of approval.

Is Your Child a Pouter?

A lot of kids pout when they don't get their way or just want attention. One of the worst things you can do is to give in to that—it only encourages them to continue. So if your kids start moping around because they can't go outside or watch a television show, politely tell them that having a bad attitude won't do them any good. And if they continue to exhibit a bad attitude, they'll lose current privileges they already enjoy.

So make your life a little easier—do without the pouting.

Are You Feeling It Ain't So Great?

In the movie *City Slickers,* Billy Crystal feels the oncoming of a midlife crisis by asking:

"Did you ever reach a point in your life when you say to yourself, 'This is the best I'm ever going to look, this is the best I'm ever going to feel, the best I'm ever going to do, and it ain't that great?'"

We've all been there. We've strived to achieve and get ahead in our careers and be honored for our accomplishments. And we wake up one day and realize "it ain't so great." What we do with that feeling of emptiness will speak volumes about our character. Will we get depressed and want to throw ourselves a pity party? Will we file for divorce and run off with the secretary? That happens more often than you think.

Or will we use the opportunity of our midlife to examine ourselves and rearrange our priorities? Will we come to the conviction that it's not all about us, but about finding fulfillment in seeing our wife and kids flourish? You see, an all-pro dad does not find his real status in a board room or a golf course, but in a sandbox and a tree fort. What you pass on to your kids—that's success. And it's a better return than any 401(k) will ever be able to offer.

Twenty-Eight Years Too Late

According to The History Channel, after twenty-eight years of his hiding in the jungles of Guam, local farmers discovered Shoichi Yokoi, a Japanese sergeant who was unaware that World War II had ended. Left behind by the retreating Japanese forces, Yokoi went into hiding rather than surrender to the Americans. In the jungles of Guam, he carved survival tools and for the next three decades waited for the return of the Japanese and his next orders. What incredible perseverance! But it was all for naught because he didn't know what was happening in the society around him. The same principle can be true for dads who want to be better fathers. You can have incredible intentions, but if you're unaware of what's going on in your child's world (their friends, music, school, and so on), then all your effort will be for naught.

So how do you enter your child's world? Spend lots of top-quality time together with him or her.

Harry Truman: A True Example of Perseverance

While he was a struggling politician, Harry Truman locked himself in a hotel room and wrote this in a personal letter:

> I know that through politics I can help people. . . . but I'm surrounded by such corruption that at times the depression sinks into me and the conflict tears into me; the headaches are terrible. But I know I'm doing right, even though it's tough.

Fatherhood can be pretty tough too. No one promised it would be an emotional walk in the park. But know that the struggles you have as a dad aren't in vain—you're building a legacy for the next generation. Don't give into fear, rather *persevere*.

Are Credit Cards Maxing Out Your Family Life?

The prolific writer, G. K. Chesterton said, "There are two ways to get enough. One is to accumulate more and more; the other is to desire less." This is especially true for your family's finances, and specifically high-interest debt. If you have outstanding interest payments, such as credit cards, your number one priority should be to get rid of that debt before you purchase more or take an extravagant vacation. Desire less, and you'll have more!

Think Being President Is Tough?

According to a Chinese proverb, "It is harder to lead a family than rule a nation."

Why? Because even political leaders can have public and private personas. But a father is a father all the time. This includes not only being a dad at the birth of your child or at his or her high school graduation, but being a dad when you have the flu, when paying the phone bill, or when pressure cleaning the driveway. Everything you are is exposed on a daily basis to your family. And while it's non-stop hard work, it's worth it all.

The Invention of the BAND-AID®

In 1921, Earle Dickson had a problem—his wife kept injuring herself in the kitchen. It frustrated him because after wrapping her wounds, the bandages would fall off shortly thereafter. So he stuck some gauze in between adhesive tape and sterilized it. He was so proud of his invention that he showed it to his boss, James Johnson, who ran Johnson & Johnson. Over eighty years and one hundred billion BAND-AID® Brand Adhesive Bandages later, you can thank Earle's thoughtfulness for his wife the next time you slam your fingernail with a hammer.

Some great ideas are birthed by love.

How Can One Be Bored with *Lord of the Rings*?

If you and your children haven't seen the film trilogy, *Lord of the Rings*, you're really missing out. Not only are the special effects stunning, but also the plot and characters are more than just skin-deep. The movie portrays the epic struggle between good and evil, with good overcoming in the end. So get your whole family involved in the series, discuss the elements of the movie, and find the symbolism.

Or better yet, read the original books together.

"ALL-PRO DAD is just what fathers today are looking for. It gives dads the hands-on help they need in a way that's practical, motivational and real. ALL-PRO DAD can make you a better father."

—Jon Kitna, Quarterback 2001–2003—
Cincinnati Bengals; 1997–2000—Seattle Seahawks

Jon Kitna met his wife, Jeni, at Central Washington University and was married on August 13, 1994. When Jon finished college he taught at a local high school before he was picked up as a free agent with the Seattle Seahawks. Jeni, also a teacher, continued to work at a high school while Jon commuted to Seattle.

The next year Jon was sent to Barcelona, Spain to play in the World League. After Jon and Jeni returned home, their boy, Jordan, was born on October 30, 1997. Following Jordan came two more children—Jalen and Jada. That's a lot of J's in the Kitna family! In addition, Jon and Jeni are the legal guardians for two teenage cousins—Chris and Casy.

Even though Jon quarterbacks in the NFL, he is the playmaker in his kids' lives. He says: "My kids wake up and make a new game every day. They are a true joy." Jon greatly admires his own father. Jon, speaking of his father, states that he "would sacrifice a lot of personal desires for me and my brother. My dad didn't have a father and wanted to do the exact opposite of what his own father had done to him—to be there."

In addition to ALL-PRO DAD, Jon and Jeni are a part of a Christian-based ministry that ministers to teenagers at Remann Hall in Tacoma. Jon is a playmaker on the field, in his community, and more importantly, as a husband and father.

What Does Your Daughter Really Want?

K en Canfield of the National Center for Fathering has done research and found the top five things daughters want from their fathers.

1. Daughters long to hear their fathers communicate love and encouragement.
   - "The best thing my dad has ever done for me is let me know he loves me."
   - "When my dad encourages me, I feel as though I could do anything."
   - "I wish my father would say, 'I love you.' "
2. Daughters want their fathers to take time to strengthen their relationship.
   - "I wish my daddy wouldn't work so much and would spend more time with me."
   - "If I could add one thing to our relationship, I would add time."
3. Daughters want their dads to communicate with them more and give them guidance.
   - "If we talked more truthfully, we would have a better relationship."
   - "I wish my dad would talk to me more and give me advice."
   - "I need more input from my dad."
4. Daughters want their fathers to seek to understand them.
   - "Sometimes I feel like my father has no idea what I'm going through."
   - "I wish my father would try to understand me."
5. Daughters want their fathers to trust them more.
   - "If I could add one thing to our relationship, I would add trust."
   - "I wish my dad would trust me more."

© 2003 by The National Center for Fathering

Do You Have the "No Personality" Mentality?

Do you punish your children not so much for doing wrong but because of their personality traits? Some children are born more naturally excited, loud, or fidgety, and this can drive some parents up the wall. And disciplining your children just for being who they are only stirs up more trouble. Here's the challenge—find constructive ways to serve as outlets for your child's challenging disposition. This could be enrolling them in sports, art class, or simply safe projects to do at home. Talk to your wife about your child's personality traits and do a little research on what kinds of activities would be beneficial for them. Sending your kids to their room all the time just won't cut it.

The Three Discipline Basics for Your Children

Do you know the three discipline basics for your children?

- The first is nonnegotiable discipline. Establish clear consequences for misbehavior ahead of time—then stick to them.
- The second is private discipline. Don't embarrass your children in front of others. Save it for the privacy of home.
- The third principle is calm discipline. Don't get so angry that you go overboard on correction or say things to your children that ultimately won't encourage them.

For a free info sheet on discipline basics, go to http://www.allprodad.com/6disciplinebasics.asp.

Does Your Child Struggle with Reading?

If one of your children seems to really struggle with reading, it doesn't automatically mean he or she is less intelligent than your other children or their classmates. In fact, many of history's brightest scholars had issues with reading and writing. Here are some key attributes to look for in a reading disorder—poor recognition of the written word, very slow reading, many mistakes in oral reading, and not understanding what one reads.

If your child experiences some or all of these, you may want to contact a physician, therapist, or school counselor for more information.

Do You Use the "Double F" Factor?

When you talk to your kids about serious subjects like premarital sex or drug abuse, remember the "Double F" factor. That means be *Frank* with the subject and *Frequent*.

Frank means being honest and to the point. In other words, no beating around the bushes—don't water down your message or allow your kids to get bored.

Frequent means you bring it up with them time and time again but from different angles. Perhaps a movie you saw together or a mutual friend or a host of things that can provide real-life illustrations of what happens when kids step outside the lines.

So when approaching difficult subjects, remember the "Double F" factor.

Do You Have a Problem with Foul Language?

Golf shots that slice far into the rough or the infamous hammer hitting one's thumbnail can unleash a stream of profanity. And those reactions are not harmless. Kids notice when their dad uses improper language, and they have a tendency to add those words to their own vocabulary—especially when dad's not around. So if you're using bad language, put a stop to it. And if a curse word slips out, apologize to your kids and tell them the reason why you shouldn't have said it.

Cursing is no small matter.

Sometimes Stating the Obvious Isn't the Best Solution

One of the dangers fathers can fall into is being too quick to lecture and too slow to listen. An example would be if your daughter feels a bit uneasy about entering middle school this fall. A typical male answer would be that millions of people have gone through middle school and turned out fine—and she will too. While that may be true, that does nothing for your daughter. Instead, letting her know that you love her unconditionally no matter what happens will give her the encouragement and strength to face her fears head on.

Have You Ever Heard of a Purity Ring?

It's a really awesome idea for teenage girls. Here's how it works—you take your daughter out to an extra fine restaurant for dinner and then talk to her about the importance of remaining sexually abstinent until marriage. You don't have to simply emphasize how remaining pure will ensure that she doesn't have an unintended pregnancy or sexually transmitted disease, but also stress that remaining a virgin will help her attain her dreams and keep her from being emotionally scarred. Tell her any man who doesn't respect her virginity wish doesn't deserve to be in a relationship with her. Ask her to make a commitment to virginity. Then, as a symbol of the evening, you give her a "purity ring." A special ring on her finger will remind her of the night's events and what you two have discussed. This will serve to continually reinforce the importance of waiting, the importance of her commitment, and the importance of your love for her.

Of course, this isn't just limited to daughters. You can do something similar (and maybe a little more masculine) for your sons. It will be a night for all to remember.

What's Coming out of
Your Teen's "Cakehole"?

Have slang words like "phat," "jacked-up," "bling-bling," and "front'n" invaded your teenager's vocabulary? If so, you're probably feeling a bit lost. And though you both may be speaking English, you're not speaking the same language. But there's a way to communicate that always breaks through—praise. By praising and encouraging your teen, by finding and pointing out the good, you'll start a communication revolution.

So make a concerted effort to point out your teen's "mad skillz" so you both can start giving each other "props."

Dads and Denial:
A Lethal Combination

Comedian George Carlin once quipped, "In Los Angeles there's a hotline for people in denial. So far no one has called." This is a humorous but also a profound insight. It's very easy as a father to live in denial about how your children are really doing. It's common to see on the news that an adolescent has been convicted of a crime and the parents claim,

"There's no way our baby could do such a thing."

This is classic denial. So be honest with yourself and with your kids. Ask your wife how she thinks the kids are doing. Look at your kids' friends. Are they a good or bad influence? Is there real communication between you and your children? Denial is the death knell for dads. Do everything you can to steer clear of it.

Cheating Is a Widespread Problem

A Josephson Institute of Ethics survey of twelve thousand high school students showed that students admitted that they cheated on an exam at least once in the past year. This percentage has continued to jump—from 61 percent in 1992 to 74 percent in 2002.

The primary reason? Many young people today believe the ends justify the means—that if you want to make a good grade on a test and if you need to cheat to do it—that's OK. But it's not OK. Character is always defined by doing the right thing, not the easy thing. So talk to your children about why cheating is wrong. Tell them that taking shortcuts will harm them in the end. Tell them you would be proud if they received only a C in a class the right way (and they did their best) rather than getting a good grade that's truly not theirs.

Got an Adolescent Going through the Curse of Zits?

D id you know that acne is not caused by poor hygiene or eating chocolate? And do you know the difference between "open comedones" and "closed comedones"? (Sounds like a dessert, doesn't it?) Getting the facts straight for your children's acne is important. Having them scrub their faces five times a day is not the answer. For a free info sheet on teenage acne, visit http://www.allprodad.com/7teenageacne.asp.

Is Your Kids' Homework Really That Important?

In the end, does it really matter what time Train A gets to the station or how many pieces of fruit are left in a basket? According to the National Center for Fathering, absolutely. They say, "Homework is about a lot more than geometry, biology, and language arts. It's an opportunity for kids to learn, sometimes the hard way, how to follow directions, prioritize their time, focus their attention, persevere through difficulties, apply research skills, and solve problems. These are all valuable life skills, and we need to be right there to help them make the most of that time."

© 2003 by The National Center for Fathering

Are Your Kids Counterculture?

Being "counterculture" doesn't necessarily mean having nose-rings and green hair. It means that they think differently than the "instant-gratification" society we live in. They weigh their decisions before they make them. They think about what's right rather than try to feel their way through it. But being counterculture must be taught by parents—it's usually not acquired elsewhere. So as a father, you need to teach your kids right from wrong and how to evaluate the situations your children find themselves in. And by taking the effort to do this, you'll be counterculture yourself!

Adopting Children You May Never Meet

Have you ever considered supporting an under-privileged child in another country? Or why not have your kids support a poverty-stricken child here in North America? There are many fine organizations—World Vision (www.wvi.org), Compassion International (www.compassion.com), or AMG International (www.amginternational.org)—through which, for modest monthly support, you can feed, clothe, and educate a child. In addition, your kids can exchange letters with the child they support to learn more about their culture and what it means to truly give for the sake of giving. Your kids will get a firsthand glimpse at what abject poverty truly is and how they can make a difference—a valuable education in itself.

Framing a Great Memory

Has your elementary-age child done something particularly well recently? If so, present him or her with a certificate of achievement. This is a wonderful, inexpensive way to make your child feel special. After you make a presentation of this certificate in front of the entire family, walk with your child to his or her room and hang it on the wall. Every time your child looks at it, he or she will remember how you went out of your way to recognize him or her for a job well done.

Teaching Life Skills Is Important Too

If you're the parent of a preteen or teenager, you're probably doing all you can to help them prepare academically for the challenges of college or the workforce after they graduate from high school. But have you prepared them with life skills? It's sometimes easy to forget to teach kids basic life survival because it's not that glamorous. But all teenagers should know how to prepare meals, do laundry, budget their money, and perform basic car maintenance among other things. Many nineteen-year-olds fresh out of the house survive off of cereal and ravioli and haven't given the oil level in their car a second thought.

So teach your kids life skills that will last a lifetime.

Want to Get Two Great Things Accomplished at Once?

To take care of two important tasks at one time, why not take your kids out shopping for a special present for Mom? It doesn't have to be her anniversary or Christmas— just a nice token of appreciation for how much she sacrifices for the family each and every day. It will make her day and allow you to spend some great quality time with your kids. So clean out the minivan, load up the kids, and head out to the mall this weekend. It will be time and money well spent.

TV Dinner

Is the television remote control sharing space with forks and knives at your dinner table? Who joins your family at mealtime? Alex Trebeck? Tom Brokaw? Sponge Bob? One study found that 44 percent of families watch television during meals. So instead of Billy talking to Mom, he's listening to Chris Berman. And Dad can't pay attention to Sally because "Money Market" is on. The point is, eating together as a family—minus the TV—is an ideal time to reconnect with each other. Make a game of it. Ask the kids current events questions. Or let them ask you about your childhood or school days. So turn off the tube, and tune into each other.

Ever Thought about Doing a Weekend Excursion with Each of Your Children?

Establish an annual tradition in which you take each of your kids on a modest weekend trip wherever they would like to go. Camping or a theme park would be a great idea. This is a superb way to build lasting memories with your kids that they'll remember all their lives. They probably won't recall the nuisances associated with travel, only that their father loved them enough to take a weekend out of the year just for them.

Are You One of Those Fathers Who Has a Loose Definition of Time?

Do you say you'll be there at 5 o'clock when the actual range could be a half hour earlier or later depending on what else is going on? While it may not be a big deal to you, if you're consistently running a half hour late in picking up your kids or attending their sporting events, you're giving the impression that whatever you were doing was more important than keeping your commitment to them. Of course, things come up occasionally when you genuinely can't make it on time, but it's important to be as punctual as you can when it involves your children.

Your time with them goes by so quickly. Be there for every minute of it.

Your Wife's Nutritional Needs

Let's look at a couple of specifics of how you can help your wife.

First, your wife needs to be taking in 800 milligrams of calcium every day to help prevent bone loss—and she needs to start now if she hasn't already. If she waits until osteoporosis sets in, it will be too late. She can obtain calcium from low-fat cheeses, milks, yogurts, and some vegetables and nuts.

Also, if your wife is consuming more saturated fat than she should be, she's greatly increasing her risk of breast cancer and heart disease. Because of this risk, less than one-third of her daily fat intake (less than 10 percent of total calories) should come from saturated fats. In addition, ingesting thirty-five grams of fiber a day through vegetables and fruit can help your wife fight off some cancers and lower cholesterol levels.

Keep your wife and your marriage relationship as healthy as it can be!

When's the Last Time You Went Cruisin' for Love?

Have you and your wife ever gone on a cruise? If not, you should really consider it. Plan to go by yourselves or with close friends. Either way, you'll spend a lot of time together in a relaxing atmosphere. Cruises are usually quite economical, and it'll be a blast to boot! Many 7-day cruises can be had for less than $600 a person.

So set sail for romantic adventure—it'll be a lot better ride than your first "bucket of bolts" you had as a teenager.

Do You and Your Wife Have a Cause?

Do your wife and you have a charitable organization that you both get behind and support? This doesn't mean just financially, but with your time and heart. There are many excellent nonprofit organizations that do tremendous work and are looking for people to rally behind them. And not only will you be helping others, but you'll also find you're growing closer to your spouse with your common cause. So whether it's helping young kids battle cancer or helping feed the homeless, find something for you both to be a part of. In helping others, you both will truly be helping yourselves.

A Soft Answer Turns Away Wrath

When you and your wife start disagreeing and things start heating up, what do you do? *Speak softly.* You can get your points across without yelling. Speaking in a quieter voice will help bring peace to the situation and encourage honest and fruitful dialogue that will help you both reach an acceptable conclusion. Screaming matches never get anywhere—they only crush feelings.

Turn down your volume and turn up solutions.

Let Her Help Shoulder the Load

If it has been one of those days where stress has built up to the point you feel you're about to explode, heed a little friendly advice. Call your wife before you get home and let her know what you're up against. This will accomplish two things.

Number one, she'll know to take it a little easy on you when you come through the front door. This will help avert a potential meltdown should she want to bring up topics you're just not able to handle right then.

Secondly, she'll feel very honored and grateful that you opened up to her and will want to help you in anyway she can. Women love shared feelings—even when the feelings aren't always great.

Let your wife help comfort you during dark days. It's a privilege she loves.

Gotten into a Little
Trouble Recently?

Hey, guys—do you want to knock your wife's socks off and maybe get yourself out of the doghouse?

Put together a list of fifteen reasons why you married her and why you would do it all over again, in addition to saying you're sorry. Leave the note on the kitchen counter with a few roses. Too often husbands, when they feel something is out of order in their marriage, will just stop by the store and pick up the first thing they see and give it to their wife. But your wife wants you to think about her and to tell her specific things you really appreciate about her. And be clear about what you did wrong as well.

Give it a try. And enjoy life outside the doghouse.

Remember That
One-Hit Wonder?

How's this for romancing your wife? Do you have a favorite song that you specifically remember her by? It could be one that was playing when you first saw her or the song you first danced to. There's no doubt that music plays a special role in our lives, and this is especially true in our marriages. So on the way home tonight, swing by a local music store and pick up a copy of that special song. It will be music to her ears.

*"Fathers want someplace to turn to get the advice
and encouragement they need to be better dads.
ALL-PRO DAD provides this valuable service."*

—Shelton Quarles, Linebacker 1997–2003—
Tampa Bay Buccaneers

Shelton Quarles is a man of perseverance.
Consider the fact that he spent several years
in the Canadian Football League before joining the Tampa
Bay Buccaneers—or how dedication to his academics
allowed him to be inducted into the National Honor
Society. But more significantly, he had to persevere in his
growing up years since his father was not around.

"I had to look for good qualities in other adults that I
could apply to my life," says Shelton. And one major source
of his inspiration was his mother. "She was like both a
mother and father to me. She provided me with the opportunity to persevere and the stability to keep trying."
Through his mother, his faith, and his life experiences,
Shelton was shaped into the outstanding player and man
that he is today. And this carries over into his role as a husband and father.

Shelton and his wife, Damaris, have a wonderful marriage. "Good communication is the best thing for us," says
Shelton. "It helps us to overcome problems and take each
other's feelings into consideration."

Shelton and Damaris also have three bundles of joy in
their children. According to Shelton, the key to being a good

dad is "trying to be tender and loveable at all times. I'm always there for my kids, and they know and enjoy that."

Shelton and Damaris are involved in Big Brothers/Big Sisters and many other charities. In addition to football, Shelton loves golfing and bowling. He says he averages around 180 on the lanes, but he didn't share his link scores—and we were a little afraid to ask. Despite his many activities, Shelton's family always comes first. And given his gift of perseverance, we know this is a commitment he'll keep.

A Father's Relentless Love

A few years ago a severe earthquake hit Turkey. Many buildings and homes were leveled. Among the thousands of casualties, a six-year-old boy named Armand was missing. His father, knowing his son was at school during the time the earthquake hit, raced to the collapsed structure. Climbing to the top of the pile, he began to pull off the shattered mud bricks. The sharp corners of the bricks sliced up his hands as he carried them down the pile and tossed them aside. He continued to off-load the bricks. Every time people would try to stop him and tell him it was useless, he would reply,

"Join me or leave me alone! Join me or leave me alone!"

After forty-seven hours of consecutive digging, he heard a voice, "Daddy, is that you?"

Armand's father exploded with joy as he found his son along with his classmates huddled together under collapsed walls. Armand kept telling his school companions,

"I told you my daddy would come! I told you my daddy would come!"

And indeed he came—a father's relentless love.

All Is Well with Dontrelle

Dontrelle Willis, an outstanding rookie pitcher who led the Florida Marlins to the 2003 World Series championship, was recently reunited with his father, whom he had not seen in nineteen years. Dontrelle arranged the get-together. His father had left home when Dontrelle was two and didn't even know he was a baseball player. Recapping the meeting, Dontrelle said, "I figured it was about time. I gave him a handshake and a hug—we tried to catch up the best way we could. It was like talking to one of my friends." Dontrelle embodies what many men are looking for today—reconnection with their dads. If you're a father who has been separated from your kids for quite some time, make a concerted effort to be a part of their lives. And while your children might not be all-star pitchers, you can definitely be an all-pro dad.

Dark Matter

Ever heard of dark matter? No, not the kinds of meals your wife served you during your first year of marriage. Physicists now believe most of the universe is composed of material that we can't see or feel. But it's there nonetheless. How do we know? Because we can detect its gravity. And dark matter seems to be the biggest factor in determining the direction and speed of the universe.

So what in the world does this have to do with fathering? A father's love can't be put on a scale or slid under a microscope. But it indeed does have weight—it has gravity. And a father's love is one of the biggest determining factors in the direction of his children's lives.

Taking Some Tonic

Here's another example of a popular band lamenting about a poor relationship with their father. The newest release of platinum-selling band, Tonic, includes a song called "Take Me As I Am." The lyrics are the words of a person who never knew his father and experienced hurt as a result of that emptiness in his life. Tonic is just one of many bands that have a common theme—absent fathers contributing to serious emotional hurt and pain.

Be physically and emotionally present for your kids.

Broken on the Pillow

Thomas Watson, an author who lived a couple hundred years ago, said the following in *The Godly Man's Picture:* "How soon are we broken on the soft pillow of ease! Adam in paradise was overcome, when Job on the dunghill was a conqueror."

You know, it's not the easy times that test your heart; it's the hard ones. It's the times when you don't know if you can make this month's mortgage, the times when your kids are sick, and the times when your wife and you seem to be continually at odds. Life is full of trials. But such trials will strengthen and help you become a better person. No matter what difficult circumstance you're in right now, with God's help, you can get through them. And if we can help at all, please e-mail us at info@allprodad.com.

Parenting Words of Wisdom
from "Mr. Chicken"

Chick-Fil-A founder, Truett Cathy, says that it's a lot better to set an example as a parent than to set a lot of rules. Anyone can lay down a bunch of regulations, but only a true man and father can live the life he wants exemplified in his children. Truett takes his parental philosophy and applies it to his corporation, which probably explains why Chick-Fil-A has experienced such phenomenal success. And this success, in spite of the fact that all its restaurants are closed on Sundays. Cathy believes Sunday is a day for faith and family. We tip our hat to Cathy and his organization— he is truly setting a great example.

The Golden Hurricane
with the Golden Heart

Ellis Jones, a standout offensive lineman at the University of Tulsa, passed away recently. Jones played for the Golden Hurricanes (1942–1944) and twice went to the Sugar Bowl and once to the Orange Bowl.

"He was one of the best football players I ever saw in that he absolutely worked at full speed all the time," said former Tulsa teammate and All-American quarterback Glenn Dobbs.

But what made Jones so special was not all the strength and skill he had but what he didn't have. His right arm was amputated eight inches below the shoulder after an accident when he was eleven.

"It never occurred to me that I couldn't keep playing football," he later told the *Tulsa World*. "I guess I was too dumb to think I couldn't do it."

If being dumb means *determining to succeed despite a handicap,* I think we could all use a little less intelligence.

Kids Can Take
Moving Pretty Hard

If you're going to be moving to a different city anytime soon, be prepared for the fact that your kids
will probably take it quite traumatically. Children
love security, and whenever they move, they must
leave their friends, their school, and many other
familiar things.

So first, explain to them why the family needs to
move and that Daddy and Mommy will still be there
to love them. Encourage them to stay connected with
their friends by giving them the new telephone number and mailing address. E-mail is also a great way
to stay in contact.

Next, have your children check the Internet
about the new city you're moving to. Have them find
out about the geography, history, climate, and amusement activities. Turn it into an adventure.

Then have your kids start packing some of their
own things so they feel they're contributing to this
moving venture.

Last, let them know it's OK to be sad and afraid
of moving, but assure them they'll meet new friends
and that soon their new place will feel like home.

There's a Difference between Bribing and Rewarding Your Kids

Bribing is giving your kids something for a task they should be doing already to avoid a potential showdown. This is particularly dangerous, because the bribe gifts will have to get larger and larger to keep up with your children's demands.

Rewards are recognition for what your kids have done that goes above and beyond what they should do. For instance, challenge your kids to learn the Bill of Rights (even if their school doesn't require it), then take them out for ice cream when they've completed the challenge.

A bribe versus a reward is an important distinction to make in motivating your kids in proper behavior.

Dads in the Workplace

There's no doubt that doing your job and doing it well has a significant, positive impact on your family. So what's essential in climbing that corporate ladder? Management guru Jim Collins studied eleven of the most successful American companies over the past fifteen years. These businesses averaged over seven times the stock returns of the general market. The most significant attribute about these businesses, Collins discovered, is that *each one* of them had unassuming, humble CEOs. Collins shares that the starting point of a great company is a humble leader. So if you want to succeed at work and at home, start with humility.

As Jesus Christ said, the last will be first, and the first will be last.

What's Your Accent?

Sixty-one-year-old Tiffany Roberts of Indiana has developed "foreign accent syndrome," a rare side effect of the stroke she suffered. Simply put, Tiffany now involuntarily speaks with a British accent even though she has never been to England nor wishes to sound like a member of the Royal Family. Tiffany has accepted her new voice and looks forward to a good life ahead of her.

This medical mystery is a great example of how children can speak differently after emotional trauma. Oh, you may not be able to detect a different pitch in their voice, but you can detect a different tone. And their words will be decidedly more negative and will be directed on how fat or ugly or stupid they are.

Don't let your kids talk about themselves that way. Keep digging to the root of their problem. It may be as simple as a slur hurled at them by a good friend or a much more serious matter. And as you help your children unfold their pain, make sure your language is accented with love and grace.

Want to Avoid Raising Bratty Kids?

We've all seen them—little, undisciplined Napoleons who want what they want and defy authority. They're dreaded by adults, feared by peers, and they're on their way to a very crummy life. Parents who always give into the wishes of their children and think their disobedience is cute are dead wrong. It's not cute to the teachers who have to teach them. It's not cute to their classmates, and it won't be cute to their future spouse and kids.

If you're not requiring your children to obey your rules, you're not only building up your own aggravation, you're doing a great disservice to your kids. Don't take the easy way out; enforce your standards and don't look the other way. Don't allow permissiveness come back to haunt you.

Sweet to the Soul

As a father, you may be focusing on saying positive and uplifting things to your kids. But are you also focusing on what your children are saying to each other? There's no doubt about it—kids can and will be mean to their siblings. So, dads, make sure your kids treat each other with respect—just like they should be treating you with respect. Point out the mean things your kids may be saying to each other, and if they won't stop, discipline them appropriately. And continue to encourage them to speak positively to each other.

As Proverbs 16:24 says, "Pleasant words are a honeycomb, sweet to the soul and healing to the bones."

Has Your Child Reached out to Someone Only to Find Themselves Rejected?

Some of our most poignant memories growing up are the times we make ourselves vulnerable only to be humiliated. Your children will go through the same thing. So how do you encourage them when this happens?

First, wrap your arms around them and tell them how much you love them. Next, tell them that unfortunately there are mean people out there and that you had to face the same thing growing up. Express to them that times of rejection are normal for everyone. Then let them know how wonderful they are and how there are many people who love them and want to be with them—starting with you.

Mentoring Your Daughter

A re you having trouble connecting with your preteen or teenage daughter? As a man, it can be quite challenging to keep a strong relationship with your daughter as she's facing issues and situations unique to young women. The situation can become even more tenuous if your wife is also not able to connect with her. A great way to reestablish that relationship may be through a female mentor for your daughter. A young woman, between the ages of eighteen and twenty-five, can break through to your daughter and help her see things in a new and positive light. Plus, the mentor can relay to you some issues your daughter may be struggling with as well as some ideas on how you can have a stronger relationship with her.

So don't be afraid to seek out a mentor at a local church, YWCA, or community organization. She can work wonders.

Teens and Alcohol Don't Mix

Underage drinking not only has its inherent health problems for teenagers, it also can be a gateway to other dangers. According to a new study released by The Henry J. Kaiser Family Foundation, teens that use alcohol are seven times more likely to have sex than kids who refrain from alcohol. Those who use illegal drugs are five times more likely to have sex than young people who don't take drugs. Teens that use alcohol are also twice as likely to have sex with four or more partners.

So, dads, be very aware of the dangers of teenage drinking. Because alcohol is not the only health issue your kids will deal with.

Never Get to Spend Much One-on-One Time with That Busy Teenager of Yours?

Maybe you're frustrated by how little time you get to spend exclusively with your teenager. How about a morning or two each week set aside for breakfast together? You can do this either in your home or at a restaurant. It's a great way to share a meal together and talk about what's going on in each other's lives. Busyness is one of the biggest obstacles parents face in connecting with their teens.

So remedy that situation over a Belgian waffle or bowl of Fruit Loops.

Adolescents and Anorexia (part 1)

According to the National Center for Fathering, a growing number of children, especially girls, fret about their body image. A poll conducted by Lou Harris Interactive found that 17 percent of girls ages eight and nine, and almost one-third of the girls ages ten to twelve, perceive themselves as overweight. That compares with 16 percent of the eight- and nine-year-old boys and 20 percent of the ten- to twelve-year-old boys.

© 2003 by The National Center for Fathering

Understand that your children may struggle with their self-image and may be at risk for anorexia. Understanding the risk is the first step in preventing it. For a free information sheet on anorexia, visit http://www.allprodad.com/7anorexia.asp..

Adolescents and Anorexia (part 2)

What are some of the causes of anorexia? Some researchers and parents blame images in magazines and on television, or even on school textbook drawings of girls that have become thinner through the years. New research in the *Journal of the American Academy of Pediatrics* reports that adolescents who diet a lot are influenced most by two factors: media images and what their fathers think. Among those classified as "constant dieters," the number one factor was their father's concern about their weight. Surprised? You shouldn't be! Your children's perceptions of who you think they are really does matter. For a free information sheet, visit http://www.allprodad.com/7anorexia.asp.

The World of MTV

When's the last time you watched MTV? If you start asking around, you'll find that most teenagers watch it. So, Dad, what about you? If your kids are wanting—and getting—their MTV, do you really know what they're tuning into? Why not spend an hour or so watching MTV? Take a look at several videos and MTV shows like "The Blame Game" or "Loveline"—you may be shocked at what you see and hear.

Next, talk to your kids about how MTV gives out the wrong messages about relationships, dating, and sex. Finally, discuss the right way to handle these issues in the "real world"—beyond MTV.

Waiting Up

Dad, do you wait up for your teenager?

Many a mother has slept on the couch until her kids got home. Then, she would get up and give them a good-night hug or a kiss. She did this to check for telltale signs of smoking or drinking.

One dad kept an alarm clock, set with the curfew time, next to his bed. It was the teen's job to turn it off when he came in, before the alarm sounded, thereby giving his father a chance to make sure all was well. These ideas may seem a little much to some of you, but if you have teenagers, you know it's better to protect than neglect.

Set Aside the Time

One of the coolest things about small kids is how they want to spend time with their father. They just love hanging out and doing stuff with their dads. But a lot of times they'll want to interrupt their dad while he's busy with chores or paying the bills to go out. Yes, dad, they want you to throw the football around or watch them color.

Your first inclination is to probably tell them "I can't." Instead, let them know you'll be along in a few minutes when you've finished up your project. Or better yet, set a specific time that day when you'll be all theirs. One day the time will come when your kids can't spend much time with you at all. Take advantage of the relatively short window of opportunity you now have.

How Do You Tell If Your Child Is Really Sick or Is Just Being a Whiner?

Two characteristics will tell you whether your child is genuinely sick—consistency and constancy. If he or she is constantly telling you that the same thing consistently hurts, take him or her to a medical professional. Kids by nature are usually whiners, but if they're consistently and constantly complaining about the same pain—take note. Telling them to tough it out could be dangerous to their health.

Wars and Rumors of Wars

Nothing has changed since ancient times. The world is full of evil and strife, and war always seems around the corner. It's scary for kids and doubly scary for those who have never had war explained to them by their parents. So if you haven't talked to your kids about this subject, explain to them that evil does exist and that good people must stop it. Most importantly, reinforce the principle that God has called you to protect your kids from harm and that they do not need to be afraid.

Are Your Children Unnecessarily Tattling on Each Other?

Tattling can be a thorn in the flesh for all parents! Johnny said this, Susie said that. It's enough to drive you bonkers. There are some definite steps you can take to curb tattling, but realize that the reason your children may be doing it is just to get attention from you. So reinforce to them that they don't need to tattle to get that desired attention. Instead, give them better ideas on how you both can spend time together.

More on Tattling

Even though a majority of tattling takes place to get attention and is not appropriate, when your children do tell on each other, you can use it in a positive way. Ask them what they think should be done about it. See what they say. And if they can't justify why they tattled, this will discourage them from doing so in the future.

Hugs

Think hugs don't matter to your children? Think again. An increasing amount of research on animals is determining that physical affection appears to play a role in maintaining brain chemistry and memory. Research is also showing children who have been deprived of positive touch have abnormal stress systems. So make sure you give your kids hugs—it's good for both you and them!

A Grief Observed

"My son, a perfect little boy of five years and three months, had ended his earthly life. You can never sympathize with me; you can never know how much of me such a young child can take away. A few weeks ago I accounted myself a very rich man, and now the poorest of all."

Ralph Waldo Emerson spoke these words after the death of his firstborn son. There are really no words to capture what a tragedy it is to lose a child. All we can do is trust that God is good and that he will provide the strength to get through our darkest hours. And he has promised that he will.

"When we look at our country and see all of the gaps that need to be filled, we naturally look for help from places like government and schools. But if dads in our country would make a commitment to their children, not just financially but also spiritually and physically—reading to them, hugging them, just loving them—then I really believe America could again reclaim its greatness. ALL-PRO DAD helps fathers fill the gap."

HOF 98

—Mike Singletary, Linebacker and Member of the Football Hall of Fame 1981–1992—Chicago Bears

Mike Singletary is a Hall of Fame football player and a hall of fame father. Mike and his wife, Kim, have seven children: Kristen, Matt, Jill, Jackie, Brooke, Becky, and John. Mike himself was the last of ten children in his family. Along the way, while growing up in a ghetto in Houston, he faced many challenges that would shape the football player and father he was to become.

Mike hit his lowest point when he was twelve. Mike's father left the family, and Mike's older brother Brady, to whom he was very close, was killed by a drunk driver. Mike says before his brother died, he told Mike to always do his best. After that, Mike made a vow that he would do just that.

He started working harder in school and in football, and he rededicated himself to his Bible study. Mike went on to play college football at Baylor University and then signed with the Chicago Bears of the NFL. After twelve seasons and ten trips to the Pro Bowl, "Samurai Mike" retired.

In 1998 he was inducted into the Pro Football Hall of Fame. The words his wife spoke at the ceremony are a testimony to the kind of father Mike Singletary is: "His induction to the Pro Football Hall of Fame is an incredible honor. But I know that Mike will consider himself a success only when each of our children, after they're grown, will look back on their relationship with Mike and name him to the 'Fathers' Hall of Fame.'"

Self-Help or Spouse Help?

I t's an interesting mark of today's society that one of the first things we encounter when we walk in a bookstore is the "Self-help" or "Self-esteem" section. Feeling good about ourselves seems to be a big business these days. But when's the last time you saw a bookstore section devoted to *spouse esteem,* or a section on *making your spouse feel cherished and loved*?

It seems sometimes that we're so focused on how we can be happy that our concern for making our wives happy only occurs when we have some extra time to spare. A real all-pro dad is far more concerned with his wife's emotional well-being and will do all he can to ensure her happiness, regardless of whether he feels content or not. And more often than not, true happiness will itself come to us when our primary concern is for her well-being, not ours.

Right or Happy?

"You can either be right or be happy."

Thus spoke an elderly gentleman who had been married for over fifty years. His humorous way of looking at things holds a lot of truth. Husbands, what's it worth for you to feel you're right all the time? Is it worth alienating your wife? You see, marriage is give and take. Obviously, there will be times when you'll disagree with your wife. But sometimes it's better to give in for the sake of peace and to show you're flexible. By demonstrating humility, you'll be a lot happier. And so will she.

Rubbing Off on Each Other

Here's some great marital insight from Canadian journalist, Richard Needham:

> You don't marry one person—you marry three: the person you think they are, the person they are, and the person they are going to become as the result of being married to you.

If you're not very happy with the direction of your marriage, you must ask yourself if you're deliberately contributing to its demise. Your negativity definitely rubs off on your spouse—which rubs back on you—and the cycle is vicious. So if you're really interested in strengthening your marriage, start counting your blessings. There are far more positives than you realize.

The Truth about Unhappy Marriages

In a recent study from the National Survey of Families and Households, 5,232 married adults were interviewed in the late 1980s. Of those surveyed, 645 of these couples said they were "unhappily married." Five years later, these same adults who said they were unhappily married—some of whom had divorced or separated and some of whom had stayed married—were interviewed again. Nearly 80 percent of those couples that stayed together considered themselves "happily married" and "much happier" five years later. Of the couples who got divorced, only 19 percent were happy five years later.

The lesson here? Even if you're in an unhappy marriage, do all you can to make it work. Seek counsel. Seasons of marital sadness will pass, and more often than not, joy is just around the corner.

Your Anniversary Plans

What are you planning for your anniversary? The typical dinner and card? Or maybe a dozen roses? Why not think outside the box next time and do something really special? Like taking her back to the place where you proposed and tell her you would do it all over again. Or put together a list of things that have changed for the positive since you've met her—like being more sensitive to others' needs or that now your shirts and pants actually match. Whatever you decide to do—make it unique. The most important thing to her is that you've given some thought to this special day, not just checked it off your to-do list.

Put the Power of Voice Mail to Work for You

When you know your wife is not going to be at home or work, leave her a message just saying that you're thinking about her and loving and missing her. It just takes a minute, but her day will be immediately brightened. Your wife loves the thought that she's on your mind even if she's not right there with you. So start leaving some voice mails. They're daily jewels your wife will treasure.

If She Wanted My Opinion, She'd Ask for It

I've noticed a huge stumbling block in my marriage—it's when I give my wife "my advice." And it's not so much that it's bad advice (in my opinion anyway); it's that I'm giving advice at all. You see, many times when my wife starts sharing her problems with me, I immediately try to fix her problems with my advice. But that's usually not what she wants. She wants me to listen and empathize. So next time your wife is pouring out her frustrations, quit making a to-do list of advice. Instead, listen and say things like "I'm sorry to hear that" and "Is there anything I can do to help?" And then if she wants your advice, you have an open invitation to give it—and it usually won't be stamped "Return to Sender."

Here's a Scary Experiment That Might Be Worth Trying

Want to get a gauge on your kids' moral compass? Youth specialist Bob DeMoss has a great idea. Rent a movie that has some objectionable material but isn't too lewd, of course. You'll have to make a judgment call on the movie based on your children's ages and maturity level. Then get paper and pens for both you and them. Before you start the movie, put $5.00 worth of quarters on the table. Tell them that you're all going to watch this movie together. Every time they see or hear something objectionable, tell them to write it down. You do the same. For every time you have something written down that they don't, they owe you a quarter. For every time they have something written down that you don't, you owe them fifty cents. Tell them not to be silly, of course.

After the movie is over, tally up the lists. Look over what they've written down, and ask them questions about what they did and didn't write down. Also share your own list and tell them the reasons for your "objectionable" items. It's a fantastic way to help your kids learn to discern what's good and bad in the media and in life. For a free article on some of the dangers of the media, visit http://www.allprodad.com/1efficaciousentertainment.asp.

Does Your Child Easily Forget Things?

As a parent, sometimes it can be frustrating when you tell your kids over and over to bring home a certain book from school or take out the Tuesday's garbage and they always forget. It seems to go in one ear and out the other for some children. The temptation is for parents to do certain tasks themselves because it'll be less hassle. But your kids need to understand that their actions (or lack of them) have consequences. If they keep forgetting a book for homework, the lack of finished homework could result in school detention. Here are a few ideas that can help them remember.

- First, some kids remember things much better if they write them down. So buy them a little pocket calendar that they can glance at every day and see what they need to do.
- You can also have your kids repeat back to you what you told them. This will help both of you know and understand what was meant.
- You may also want to keep a kids' to-do list on the refrigerator door for that week so whenever your kids help themselves to something to eat or drink, they'll be reminded of their obligations.

Simple things to help remind them of their duties will help avoid longer, more complex arguments.

A Great Idea for the Family

Over a period of several days, videotape interviews with each family member on specific topics, such as the funniest things I've ever seen . . . some of the most embarrassing things I've done . . . or the happiest times of my life. Then gather the family together, fire up some popcorn, and watch everyone's interviews. It will be a great time of laughter and some good-natured ribbing. You may even want to record a "funny face" competition for good measure. Dad will win that hands down.

Is One of Your Kids Unpopular?

This is a tough issue for both kids and parents to face. We've all been there. We all know what it's like to go to school and be the object of scorn. And while it was painful for us to be rejected, very few things top the distress of seeing our kids being humiliated by their peers. So what do you do?

First, listen carefully to what your child is saying. Perhaps you can offer advice that will uplift his or her spirit. Then, share with your child that being teased is unfortunately a normal part of growing up. Advise your child on what he or she may be able to do to minimize teasing and make new friends. Finally, offer your unconditional love and support.

Do You Know How Many Senior Citizens Live in Nursing Homes around You?

Many older folks, after their spouse dies, don't have a network to support them. Their children might live in different states. Friends of theirs may have died or have health problems of their own. But your children can literally save their lives—physically and emotionally. One of the biggest factors older folks face is loneliness. And there's no greater joy to many seniors than having kids around. So get your kids involved in a local nursing home or assisted-living facility. They'll probably balk at first, but it can be just as rewarding for your kids as the people they will help care for.

Teach Your Kids Compassion

Use object lessons to teach your children compassion. For instance, have your family drink only water for a couple of weeks instead of soft drinks. Not only is this more healthy, but you also can use the money you would normally spend for soda and send it to a nonprofit organization that helps people dig fresh water wells in Third World countries. Or deliberately buy generic clothes instead of name-brand ones, and send the savings to help clothe orphans. Using visual examples of compassion will make a strong, lasting impression on your children.

Are Your Children's Rooms Disaster Areas?

If your children's rooms look like a nuclear bomb hit them, it's time to make them clean it up. Some parents let their kids' rooms be their kids' rooms and don't enforce the neatness standards there as they do elsewhere in the house. But it's not good for your kids to be comfortable with messiness and disorganization. Believe it or not, the messy state of their rooms can literally spill over into other areas of their lives. So if you haven't checked out your kids' rooms lately, strap on a hard hat and get busy!

Struggling with Anger

Dealing with the pressures of work and coming home to a sometimes chaotic household can tempt even the most honorable man to lash out. And we've all regretted the times we've lost our temper and said things we shouldn't have. You may need to go to another room for a little while to cool off. Breathing deeply and speaking in a calm voice will also help. Yelling at your kids won't solve anything. When you're upset with them, speak to them firmly, and back it up with discipline if need be. And be sure to have outlets for your anger, such as exercise or an enjoyable hobby. Either you'll control your anger, or your anger will control you. There's no middle road.

Take a Walk in the Park

Your wife would love to sleep in and lounge around on an occasional Saturday morning. So why don't you get up early and take your kids to a park or athletic complex? You'll be spending top-quality time with your kids, getting a great workout, and giving your wife some much-needed downtime. It can be a wonderful tradition that your kids will look forward to for years to come.

Do You Badmouth Your Children's Authority Figures?

If you're cutting down your child's schoolteacher, babysitter, pastor, or other authority figure, you're doing a great disservice to your kids. By talking negatively in front of your kids about their leaders, you're instilling disrespect and discontent into your children. You're also telling your kids, in no uncertain terms, that they don't have to respect or obey authority figures. If you have a problem with someone in your child's life, go to that person directly. By talking negatively, all you're doing is reinforcing rebellion in your kids.

Does Your Love Seem to Have Strings Attached?

Many men are accomplishment driven and judge themselves by what they're able to do. And this can translate into parenting. Some dads limit the times they tell their kids they love them to just those times when they do something well—like getting an A on a test or hitting a homerun. But do you tell your kids you love them even when they fail a quiz or strike out in the bottom of the ninth?

If your kids feel your love for them is performance-based, they'll never really have a deep relationship with you. By all means, praise them when they do things well, but, most of all, love them just for who they are.

Keeping Your Kids Safe from the Dangers of the Internet

One of the questions we're asked a lot here at Family First and ALL-PRO DAD is what we can do to protect our kids from the dangers of the Internet. There were so many inquiries, in fact, that we put together a free comprehensive guide for parents to look through and become better educated about the options out there. Visit http://www.familyfirst.net/parenting/internetguide.asp. This is good stuff. Please let us know how it helps you and your family.

Learning More about the Teachers Your Kids Learn From

If you're like most families, your children's teachers spend more time with your kids during the week than you do. But how well do you know the teachers? It would be great for you to introduce yourself to your kids' teachers and get to know them a little bit. This not only makes the lines of communication easier should the teacher need to talk to you, but it'll also give you insight as to what your child is learning as well as who is teaching them. And teachers will love the fact that a father will take the time to be involved and play an active part in his children's education.

Dads and Delinquency

According to counselor and football great, Bill Glass (who has spent twenty-five years with men who are incarcerated), not one of the thousands of prisoners he has met has genuinely loved his dad. And Dave Simmons, author of *Dad, the Family Counselor,* conducted a study that said over 90 percent of men on death row hated their fathers. The correlation between social problems and lack of fatherly affection has been established time and time again. Being a loving dad is not only crucial for your family, but it also dictates the future course of our society. Dads, you matter—to everyone. For more fatherhood statistical information, visit http://www.allprodad.com/1fatheringfacts.asp.

Teenage Pregnancy

Do you know a teenager who is pregnant? Perhaps it's your daughter, or a friend of your daughter. Pregnant teens aren't limited to the inner city. They cut across social and economic lines. Kids should be continually told by their parents to stay away from sex. Unfortunately, some teens will choose not to listen and will become pregnant. But good can still come out of it. The pregnant teen should be encouraged to read literature and even view her baby through ultrasound so she knows it's a life to be treasured. If she's unable to care for the child by herself, she can place him or her in an adopting family who will love and care for the child.

Out of the pain and shame of unwed pregnancy can come life and blessing. Do your part to help it become so.

Fathers Do Matter
to Daughters

According to the National Center for Fathering, "Recent studies have yielded some significant insights about fathers' importance to their daughters. At a surprisingly young age, girls begin to absorb society's expectations. As teens, they become vulnerable to the popular messages that focus on their bodies, their looks, and their independence. A University of Arizona study found that 90% of all teenage girls were unhappy with their weight. A parallel study noted that girls who are not affirmed by their fathers are more likely to be promiscuous and less likely to commit to long-term relationships."

© 2003 by The National Center for Fathering

If there was any doubt about how much a father matters to a daughter, recent studies prove they matter enormously.

Is Your Teenage Son
Unsure of How to Handle
Himself with Girls?

Does your teenage son think he doesn't measure up to other guys? All of us men can relate. Dating is terrifying—especially for teenage boys who don't look or act like Brad Pitt. But you know what the number-one consensus is as to what teenage girls want?

Character.

They want a man who will treat them with compassion, respect, and sensitivity. So how can your son learn that? He can start by showing all of these things to his mother. Then he's ready for dating.

Are You Dealing with an Angry Adolescent?

Many young people today are full of rage. It could be anger that's justified by a family or school situation, or it could be that they're just being rebellious. In any case, many in the media encourage this adolescent distress and ire, so as a parent you have to chart a course upstream to help their anger. First, get them to admit that they're angry and need to control this rage. Then help them to articulate their feeling without exploding. Show them practical ways to deal with rage by facing up to a situation that angers them. This is definitely a time for parental understanding and empathy.

Lovingly Relentless

If you have a rebellious teenager or worry you have one in the making, don't just passively sit back and hope they'll grow out of this stage. You need to take steps to keep them from harming themselves and your family. So what can you do when your kids aren't doing as you wish and won't even listen to you? First, make sure you pray for them. Prayer does wonders.

Second, make sure you're involved in your teen's life—from attending their high school activities to going out to eat with them. Be there!

Third, don't take "no" for an answer. When they tell you they don't want to talk about it, persevere without being pushy. Be lovingly relentless.

Fretting over Your Kids Going to College?

A re you unsure where the money is going to come from? Here are a few tips.

- First, start a special savings account, if you haven't already. You may want to consider establishing an automatic payroll deduction and have the money placed in a special educational account. Increase the amount of savings each year so it matches the college inflation rate.
- If your kids are in high school, have them do some research on scholarships.
- It also helps to see if your good old mom and dad will pitch in.
- Last, you may not want to foot the entire bill for your kids' college education. Paying for some of it themselves may help them appreciate it more.

Avoiding Date Rape

I t's unfortunate that we have to talk about the dangers of date rape, but not talking about it with your daughter is even more dangerous. Rape does happen. And it usually happens by young men that the girls are acquainted with. The best rape prevention is to make sure the guys your daughter goes out with are men of character. And this is your responsibility to judge as much as your daughter's. And while no one can know for sure what someone will be like on a date, it's certainly a good bet that parental approval will go a long way in preventing a tragedy.

"Playing in the NFL is a fantastic experience, but nothing can compare to the experience of being a father. ALL-PRO DAD helps men get the most out of this tremendous privilege."

—Jay Riemersma, Tight End 2003—
Pittsburgh Steelers; 1997–2002—Buffalo Bills

Jay knows what it's like to perform under pressure. What else could you expect from one of the NFL's premier tight ends? Catching fifteen touchdown passes over the past three seasons against the defensive prowess of aggressive linebackers takes skill and courage. But so does being a husband and a father.

Jay considers his wife Cara to truly be a blessing from God. They met in high school and have been sweethearts ever since. Jay says that they are best friends: "We have great times together and can also tackle problems together, because the center point of our marriage is faith."

Cara is a great athlete herself, having been all-state in volleyball and swimming while in high school. Jay credits Cara as "a truly wonderful wife and mother."

Jay and Cara are the immensely proud parents of a daughter, Sophia Grace. Becoming the father of Sophia has changed some of Jay's perspectives. He is now especially aware of how children will emulate and imitate their parents—both their good traits and their bad ones. Jay also says, "I now understand the kind of unconditional love my parents have for me. Growing up, I knew they loved me, but now having my own child has shed a new light on the kind of love my folks showed me. I have a newfound respect for them."

Jay says that in order for fathers to be better dads, they must understand the kind of love their heavenly Father has for them and acknowledge and embrace the accountability and responsibility dads have to be examples to their children. And while Jay continues to cradle game-winning touchdown passes, the most important use of his hands is to hold and hug his wife and daughter.

An Englishman's Advice to Fathers

Several centuries ago, William Pitt, an English statesman and orator, made the observation that:

> The poorest man may in his cottage bid defiance to all the force of the Crown. It may be frail; its roof may shake; the wind may blow through it; the storms may enter, the rain may enter, but the King of England cannot enter; all his forces dare not cross the threshold of his ruined tenement.

In other words, a home is to be the sanctuary for the family, no matter what's going on in the outside world. So how is the atmosphere at your house? Does your family find a place of refuge there? Do your children feel safe and secure? Ask your family these questions around the dinner table tonight, and see what you all can do to make your house truly a home—and a sanctuary that cannot be shaken.

Success

Are you concerned that your child may not succeed in life? Take some advice from legendary coach Bear Bryant: "I have tried to teach my players to show class, to have pride, and to display character. I think football, winning games, takes care of itself if you do that." Bryant's philosophy was simple—teach your players to be virtuous, and everything else will take care of itself.

As a father, it can be tempting to want your kids to grow up and become professional athletes or savvy businesspeople. But a father's ultimate goal should be to raise up children who will have outstanding character. That's true success. And everything else will follow after that.

Jesse Owens

There are times when a man transcends his sport and even his circumstances. Jesse Owens, born the son of a sharecropper and the grandson of a slave, ended up winning four gold medals at the 1936 Berlin Olympic Games in front of a mocking Adolf Hitler. The only way Jesse was able to overcome such odds and perform so well in front of a hostile crowd was by refusing to back down.

As a father, it's easy to get discouraged by circumstances—to look at the obstacles before you as insurmountable. Whether it's financial pressure or rebellious kids, being a dad is often difficult and thankless. But champions always transcend their situation and persevere in what is right. So remember this the next time you face a fatherhood challenge: obstacles are what you see when you take your eyes off the goal.

Have Your Kids Recently Failed at Something?

Perhaps one of your children tried out for a team and didn't make it. Maybe they failed to get into the college of his or her choice. Everyone fails! True heroes fail, often, because they're not afraid to try. Consider the following true story that may encourage your kids.

A young boy lost his mom when he was nine, was fired as a clerk when he was twenty, had no formal education, went into heavy debt when he was twenty-three, and proposed to a girl he dated for four years but was turned down. He then entered Congress when he was thirty-seven after his third try, then failed to get reelected. At forty-five he lost his Senate bid and at forty-seven lost his run for the vice presidency. At fifty-one this man then became the President of the United States. You might have heard of him—Abraham Lincoln.

Have You Passed on to Your Children the Importance of Tradition?

In his book *Orthodoxy*, G. K. Chesterton writes:

> Tradition means giving a vote to the most obscure of all classes, our ancestors. It is the democracy of the dead. Tradition refuses to submit to the small and arrogant oligarchy of those who merely happen to be walking about. All democrats object to men being disqualified by the accident of birth; tradition objects to their being disqualified by the accident of death. Democracy tells us not to neglect a good man's opinion, even if he is our groom; tradition asks us not to neglect a good man's opinion, even if he is our father.

Well put, G. K.!

Having It All?

Can you really have it all? You know—the perfect job, plenty of money, a loving wife, well-behaved children, good health, and the ability to shoot a round of 65. We're told we can "have it all," but in reality, we can't. We have limited time and resources, and we live in a fallen world where we're treated unfairly and must deal with problems and obstacles on a continual basis. Most of us will never achieve all we dreamed of doing, so we have to make choices as to where we spend our time and energy to make our most important aspirations come true. And for the all-pro dad, a beautiful family life is the dream that transcends all others our society can offer.

So You Don't Feel You're the Best Dad in the World?

So, you're not the supercool father dude on television shows. And you can't throw a football fifty yards. And you have morning breath. But what is it that your kids really need from you?

Loving consistency!

Being there for them day in and day out. Being a constant presence in your kids' lives lets them know that they do matter and are loved. So don't be intimidated that you might not be the hippest dad around—but instead, realize that you can be a great father just because you're around.

Are You Open to Correction?

n the book *Hidden Keys of a Loving, Lasting Marriage* author Gary Smalley relates the following:

> A man may resist being open to correction from his wife because he feels it somehow negates his position as the leader of the home. If he listens to his wife's complaints or suggestions to improve their relationship and acts on them, he fears it means letting his wife make every decision or giving up control of the home. Although a man may fear that responding to suggestions from his wife might 'open the floodgates' to her trying to take over their marriage, I have seen just the opposite be true. When a woman sees her husband's willingness to accept correction—a mark of someone who wants to gain wisdom—she is more willing to follow his leadership in the home because she values him more highly.
>
> ©1993 by Gary Smalley

This is great advice from Gary. If you're open to correction, you'll find your wife will be much more responsive to your needs as well.

The Grass Isn't Always Greener

Over 40 percent of first marriages, 60 percent of second marriages, and 75 percent of third marriages end in divorce. If you're thinking about leaving your wife because someone out there might make you happier, the odds are that you'll actually end up in a worse situation. Studies show again and again that couples who endure hardships together and don't bail out on their marriages almost always end up happier once they've gone through the trial.

So if times are tough right now, stick it out. As it has been said, "Weeping may endure for a night, But joy comes in the morning" (Ps. 30:5, NKJV).

One Year of Diamonds

I've heard cynics describe marriage as one year of diamonds and fifty years of charcoal. I believe this philosophy comes from relating love to feeling, not to a daily decision. The feelings of love come and go, and then return again like your appetite. The commitment of love is unrelenting and sure. Loving commitment is an act of the will— a self-disciplined lifestyle. Act in love towards your wife even if you don't always feel like it. The feelings will return and flood your soul with joy.

Do You Have Room for Disagreement?

When you and your wife get into a serious disagreement, you should take the conversation elsewhere and not carry on a fight in front of the kids. Designate an area away from the children where you can enter into "serious discussion" without your kids hearing. It makes children uneasy when parents fight and may cause them to feel they have to pick a side. Parents need to present a unified front as much as possible. So when there is a little disunity among you, work it out anywhere, but not in front of the kids.

Doing Your Best When Your Wife Has PMS

If your wife has some tough days with premenstrual syndrome (PMS), you're probably fully and totally aware of it. But how are you reacting to it? Do you get into a verbal war if she's cranky? Or do you prefer to just go and cower in the corner somewhere until it passes? Actually, the best thing you can do is support her both verbally and with actions. Compliment her. Do a load of laundry. Interact with the kids more. You'll find a lot more harmony in your marriage when you show a little extra empathy.

Take Marriage Problems
on Vacation

Having a few problems communicating in marriage but aren't quite sure how to solve them? Then go on vacation! Well, sort of.

If your marriage isn't where it should be, you should strongly consider going on a weekend retreat geared toward married couples. Problems, ideas, and suggestions can be talked out in a nonthreatening, supportive atmosphere. So don't let marital friction be a constant struggle. Book a marriage weekend retreat today. If you're having some trouble finding one, e-mail us at info@allprodad.com, and we'll be glad to help.

How's This for Marital Honesty?

You and your wife should develop a list of four things you wish the other would or wouldn't do.

- For you, you may wish that your wife wouldn't leave her shoes lying around the bedroom floor or wouldn't drive her car with low air in the tires.
- She may write down how she gets annoyed when you don't wash your whiskers down the sink or, how you always leave the seat up.

Whatever the annoying habits might be, write them down on a sheet of paper, and exchange the list with each other. This is a great way to settle nagging issues and open up some good dialogue. But be sensitive and reasonable when you put together your list. You don't want to start World War III. For a free article on solving marital conflicts, go to http://www.allprodad.com/2maritalconflicts.asp.

Finding Fantasies for Your Family

Fantasy movies seem to be hot commodities these days. But what kind of fairy tales should we let our kids watch? I'm a big fan of the right kind of fantasies—the ones that are really just extended parables. There should be clear-cut guidelines of good and evil, consequences for people's actions, and lessons learned as the heroes struggle with adversity. J. R. R. Tolkien's *Lord of the Rings* and C. S. Lewis's *Chronicles of Narnia* are two great children's fantasy series that come to mind. It's fun just to enjoy them and escape for a while.

As Tolkien once said, "Not all those who wander are lost."

Bugs Bunny and Family Life

Ever heard of the Saturday morning cartoon date? If you have children between the ages of five and twelve, you know how hard it is for parents to get some time alone together. One idea is to have your kids camp out with sleeping bags in the living room on Friday night. When they awake on Saturday morning, they get their own breakfast and are entertained by cartoons. It provides a welcome relief for mom and dad, plus a few more minutes of that valuable shut-eye.

Compliments—Pass along the Joy

It's very important for children to hear compliments—and not only from parents, but also from other adults as well. When an adult friend or acquaintance compliments your children (and the kids aren't around to hear it), be sure to pass along the said compliment to your kids. Kids already know their parents are "naturally biased," but hearing how other grown-ups recognize and appreciate them can mean a great deal. And while you're sharing other people's compliments with your kids, go ahead and add your own as well.

Turning Arguments into Discussions

When it comes to disagreements with your children, there's always the temptation to end the argument with the ubiquitous "because I said so." There may indeed be times this needs to be done, but it should not be used as a continual cop-out for vigorous discussions. Instead, be willing to listen to your kids, and let them present their case. Then you can counter with, "Well, this is what I think" or "From my experience . . ." Always attempt to move a heated discussion from the emotional to the logical. In the end, you may have to wield your parental authority if you can't convince your child, but at least they know they had the opportunity to be listened to and present their case.

College Scholarships

It's never too early to start thinking about the possibility of college scholarships. Believe it or not, some kids can obtain scholarships before they ever set foot in their local high school, let alone a college. The two keys in the scholarship search are: first, to know what's available and second, start the search early. There is a lot of educational money available, but it's essential to know where to look and what you're looking for. The administrative office at your children's school is a wonderful resource for books and scholarship information, as is the public library.

More on College Scholarships

In applying for any college scholarship, it's important to read and follow the application instructions thoroughly. It sounds simple, but many applicants are rejected because they didn't follow proper instructions. It's also much better to get letters of recommendation from people who know your children than from those who have a nice title, but know little about your kids.

Check out your local college or junior college to see if they offer scholarship seminars. This can be a great way to get hands-on help in obtaining funds for your children's education.

Help for Disorganized Kids

Some children have trouble keeping themselves together. They have to be constantly reminded to do their chores or finish their homework, and this can be a source of contention for both you and your kids. So we suggest getting a large dry-erasable calendar with markers. Hang this in a prominent place at home. Have your kids jot down on the calendar all they need to do during that month or that week or that day. Then by a quick glance, they'll know all that is expected of them. Teaching your kids to budget their time wisely and to fulfill their obligations is crucial to their future success.

When Tragedy Strikes

One of the hardest things a family has to go through is a severe illness of one of the children. Untold stress, time, energy, and money are poured into trying to deal with this tragedy. If you've been through it before, you know how tough it is. If you haven't, the best thing you can do is be prepared beforehand.

- Talk to your children's mother about getting an action plan together should your child become ill. What does your current health insurance policy cover? Do you need supplemental insurance?
- Think about friends and family who can pitch in and help with daily household chores, food, and so on for your other children. Check ahead of time with your friends to see if they'd be willing to help.
- Make use of support groups—they can provide valuable guidance as you try to unfurl exactly what's going on with your child and what the best course of action is. *Always* get a second opinion from a medical professional.
- And above all, pray.

Nothing can quite prepare you for the trauma of having a child with a serious disease, but thinking ahead will prove to be one of the best things you've done.

The Pressure of Popularity

One of the greatest pressures facing preteens and teens is the need to be popular and accepted. So many young people base their self-esteem on what their peers think of them. And when classmates reject them, kids can get seriously depressed. But as a dad, you can make all the difference in the world. You can recount to your children what it was like growing up and experiencing the feelings and pain of rejection. And how, ultimately, you became a stronger person because of it. Bathe your kids in love and encouragement. Let them know they'll find the right friends in due time. And reinforce that while popularity dynamics change, your love for them never will.

Explore What Your Kids Are Exposed To

You do all you can to provide a wholesome environment for your kids at home. But how much do you know about the environment of the homes of your kids' friends? Sometimes the parents of your children's friends allow movies and music into their house that you would object to. So it's important as a father that you understand what your children may be exposed to when they go to a friend's home. It may take a little courage to ask other parents what their standards are and to tell them what your expectations are; but in the end, taking a vested interest in everything your children may be exposed to is the responsibility of being a good dad. For more on the dangers of some forms of entertainment, visit http://www.allprodad.com/1efficaciousentertainment.asp.

Are You Easy to Talk To?

According to a Philips survey, 73 percent of kids say they spend less than one hour a day talking to their parents. Only 20 percent said it's "very easy" to talk to parents about things that really matter. That means that 80 percent of children have trouble talking to Mom or Dad about significant issues going on in their lives. So which category do your children fall under? Want to find out? Ask them. And if they tell you you're not the easiest person in the world to talk to, don't blow your stack. Instead, ask them specific ways you can improve on communication. And listen.

It's Good to Be a Chauvinist

But not the type you're thinking of. The word traces back to Nicolas Chauvin, a 19th-century French soldier who was extremely devoted to his country. In France, the name *Chauvin* came to mean anyone who was steadfastly patriotic. As time marched on, *chauvinist* came to refer to a person who is extremely attached or loyal to a particular group. Finally, the word devolved to mean someone who is a sexist.

Be chauvinistic in the right sense, as a man completely devoted to family. Seek to serve and love them. Our country needs a few good men and also, desperately, needs a few good fathers.

What Is Your Compliment-to-Criticism Ratio?

Is the bulk of your conversation with your kids telling them to knock it off or sit up straight or keep quiet? Kids are kids and by nature are squirmy, and this can, at times, be frustrating for adults. But if you're constantly criticizing your children and rarely encouraging them or telling them you love them or that you're proud of them, your kids' main goal will be avoiding you. And you don't want that. Pay attention to your children, and make a mental note to praise them—not just criticize.

Do You Constantly Feel "Trapped"?

Is it hard for you to get some personal time alone? Perhaps when you wake up your first order of business is blasting your kids out of bed to get ready for school. Then you're off to work, where you're always dealing with one problem or crisis after another. Then you come home and chat with your wife about the day's events and help your kids with their geography homework. Finally you slump into bed exhausted—only to repeat the trend the next day, and the next week, and the next twenty years.

If you don't take some time out for yourself, you could very well be headed for a midlife crisis. One of the best things you can do is to get up a few minutes earlier in the morning and pray, perhaps go for a jog, or just relax a bit. And know that it's okay, at times, to go on a camping trip with the guys or fishing with your brother. Breaking up your hectic schedule will rejuvenate you and help you be a better husband and father. Don't feel guilty about getting away from time to time. And encourage your wife to do the same.

"I never realized how important dads were until I had my own children. I was raised without a dad. You can make a huge difference in your children's lives when you're available to them. ALL-PRO DAD lets you know how to do that."

HOF 98

—Anthony Muñoz, Offensive Tackle
and Member of the Football Hall of Fame
1980–1992—Cincinnati Bengals

To understand what Anthony Muñoz is all about, you need only look in one place. No, not the NFL Hall of Fame where he was inducted in 1998. And no, not Cincinnati where Anthony played for the Bengals for thirteen years. No, to truly understand Anthony Muñoz, you need to look into his heart. There you'll find what matters to him most—his faith and his family.

During his Hall of Fame induction speech he said, "In my second year in the NFL, I knew I wasn't motivated by the money. I knew I wasn't motivated by the notoriety. I knew there had to be more to playing in the NFL. And I realized as I looked through Scripture that I was to present my body as a living sacrifice, and that was my way to worship God."

Anthony grew up in California with his mom, Esther, and his two brothers and two sisters. He gives his mother credit for raising five children on her own. He says he never realized how important a father is in his children's lives until he and his wife, DeDe, had their own children, Michael and Michelle.

In high school Anthony was a multisport standout. At the University of Southern California he was a football all-American and a member of the 1978 national championship team.

His football success continued after he was drafted in the first round by the Cincinnati Bengals in 1980. His career with the Bengals landed him on the Pro Bowl team eleven years in a row. Then he was given the ultimate honor—induction into the NFL Hall of Fame.

The day of the ceremony Anthony's son, Michael, gave the induction speech for his dad. He said, "You've taught me to let my actions speak louder than my words and to make people more important than things."

That's what Anthony Muñoz is all about. And it's why he's a member of the ALL-PRO DAD team.

Dads with Special-Needs Children Are Special Indeed

The National Center for Fathering details information about fathers of special-needs children that we all learn from. Though these fathers are more vulnerable to family and marital discord, many of these men display heroic calmness and dedication in high-stress circumstances. A research survey, along with real-life testimonies from fathers who are successful in nurturing a special-needs child reveals these characteristics:

1. They accept their child's condition and view it as a daily task with ups and downs.
2. They're more aware of their family's emotional needs and seek to contribute to a positive attitude.
3. They have learned to grieve openly and respect the feelings of other family members.
4. They've developed a network of support, which provides encouragement to their family during difficult times.

These men are heroes from whom we have much to learn.

© 2001 by The National Center for Fathering

Gill Byrd

Gill Byrd is a man who knows how to use his hands. He led the NFL in interceptions from 1987 to 1992. But nothing could prepare him as he held in those storied hands a son born three months premature. With his child weighing only two pounds, Gill vowed to protect him—even more than he would a recovered fumble or a picked-off pass. Today Gill's son is a healthy young man. The intensity and passion that made Gill a great player has also made him a great father. We are grateful he is a member of the ALL-PRO DAD team. To read his biography, visit http://www.allprodad.com/byrd.asp.

What's Most Important

World War II leader General Douglas MacArthur had this to say about what's really important:

> By profession, I am a soldier and take great pride in that fact. But I am prouder, infinitely prouder, to be a father. A soldier destroys in order to build. The father only builds, never destroys. The one has the potentialities of death; the other embodies creation and life. And while the hordes of death are mighty, the battalions of life are mightier still. It is my hope that my son, when I am gone, will remember me not from the battlefield but in the home repeating with him our simple daily prayer, "Our Father Who Art in Heaven."

What about your children? Will they remember you more for your commitment to your job than for your commitment to them? Take a tip from the general and make your children—not your job—your ultimate legacy.

She Was the Best

She was ranked the number one tennis player from 1972 to 1978. She won eighteen Grand Slam singles titles and was the first woman to reach one million dollars in career tournament earnings. But what does Chris Evert Lloyd see as her most important accomplishment? Listen to her: "The great high of winning Wimbledon lasts for about a week. You go down in the record book, but you don't have anything tangible to hold on to. But having a baby—there isn't any comparison." For all the trophies Chris Evert Lloyd has ever hoisted, none can compare to the lifting up of her children on a daily basis.

Male Role Models Are Missing in Action

According to a recent Gallup youth survey, four out of every ten American teens are living with only one of their parents. In eight out of ten cases, the absent parent is the father. Way too many men are missing in action when it comes to raising their own kids. And these teenagers need to have positive male role models in their lives. So, dads, look outside your own immediate family to some ways you might be able to help other children. From coaching a Little League team to regularly visiting a children's home to helping out at a school, you can become the example that some kids have never had before—a true man.

The Smallest Action Can Be of Greatest Importance

The magazine, *Glimpses,* relates the following story: Nathaniel Hawthorne is famed as the author of one of America's greatest novels, *The Scarlet Letter.* But it may have been a small kindness that was most influential to his daughter Rose. Nathaniel visited an English poorhouse where a diseased child rubbed his sore legs and held out hands in a plea to be lifted up. Although shrinking from the child's repulsive sores, the author picked the boy up and caressed him. Nathaniel said later that he felt as if God had promised the boy that kindness, and if he refused it, he could never call himself a man again. Hawthorne's daughter, Rose, was so influenced by her father's actions that she later started charities specifically to deal with patients suffering from cancer. Seven homes in six states are available free of charge to cancer patients because of the work of Rose and the influence of her father.

It's Funny How Good Luck Usually Follows Hard Work

There's one overriding factor in determining success in the workplace. Very rarely is luck or charisma responsible for great achievements. The cornerstone is determination— the mind-set to overcome anything in the way of your goal. Being a good dad takes exactly that—determination not to let anything get between you and your children—no matter how hard you have to work at it.

Thomas Edison said, "Opportunity is missed by most people, because it is dressed in overalls and looks like work." Being a dad is work and it's usually not glamorous, but it's well worth the effort.

Practical Tips for a Troubled Marriage

Being ever vigilant about your marriage is the key to keeping your marriage strong. We often let little things build up over time that can come back to haunt us later. One of the best guards against this is one-on-one time with your spouse. This allows time for discussion. And discussion is the key to intimacy. You need more than just a date night. You need weekends set aside for romantic getaways and a regular pattern of downtime. So arrange with close friends and family for them to look after the kids while you and your wife get away or just enjoy some quiet time at home. If your marriage is facing some struggling times, there are getaway conferences designed just for you. Visit http://www.allprodad.com/2marriageconferences.asp for a free info sheet.

Does Your Wife Like
to Be Pampered?

Why not send her to a spa during an upcoming weekend while you take the kids? Between mudpacks and
cucumber eyes, she'll get some of that much-needed downtime and come back refreshed and rejuvenated. If you can't
afford a weekend spa, then make an appointment for her
to get a pedicure. Somewhere between the marriage altar
and today, most of us have forgotten how to make our wives
feel like a princess. We married royalty—let's not forget it.

A Chivalrous Husband

Chivalry isn't dead—it's just missing in action. It's surprising how many husbands today don't provide a simple courtesy like holding the door open for their wives or
pulling out their chairs for them when they're seated. While
these things may seem quaint, they show women the respect
they deserve. So if you haven't been quite the gentleman you
should be, there's no time like the present to start. And
you'll be setting a great example for your kids as well.

Women and Divorce

A study recently published in the *Journal of Marriage and Family* focused on the question as to why marriages of adult children of divorce are more likely to end in a divorce than marriages between partners from intact families. A survey of women centered on 464 random partners:

> Compared with women from intact families, women from divorced families reported ambivalence about becoming involved . . . and more conflict and negativity in their relationships.

Researchers reported that women from broken homes were less likely to trust their partners and that this usually led to much greater difficulty in marriage. So, husbands, please realize that if your spouse comes from a divorced home, you may need to have greater sensitivity to issues such as trust and security.

Your Wife Is Beautiful

When's the last time you told your wife that she is beautiful—and without some hidden agenda? Some men are a little uncomfortable telling their wives that they're pretty because it might sound corny. But you don't have to be William Shakespeare to say something meaningful. A simple, short, heartfelt statement will suffice. A wife wants her husband to think she's beautiful just as you want her to think you're handsome. So don't hold back the compliments until you need something. Make it a constant practice, and watch what a difference it will make in your relationship.

Temptation

Think you're too strong to be tempted? Think again. Adultery happens to all kinds of men from all walks of life. The word "adultery" comes from the Latin *adalterer.* The *ad* meaning "to" and the *alter* meaning "another." Adultery is adding another person to your intimate life who has no right to be there. And the brief moments of pleasure can in no way compare to the devastation that will occur to those you should love most dearly.

The first key in staying faithful is to understand that you can be tempted. The biggest mistake is to think you're above it.

The second key is to take steps that will minimize temptation. This includes avoiding time one-on-one with another woman for an extensive period (be it in person or on the Internet) and being careful with what you watch and read. No matter how casually some television shows or movies treat adultery, it's a sin to be avoided at all costs.

Silence

Is your wife giving you the silent treatment? It's tough to take isn't it? And most men, when faced with it, will continually badger their wife trying to get her to open up. But this usually isn't the best course of action. Instead, ask her what's wrong in a calm, sincere voice. If she still won't talk, give her some space. And don't automatically assume that the problem is with you. Just let her know you love her and want to do what's best to keep the communication lines open in your marriage. There are times when you give her the silent treatment too, so just think about how you would like to be treated—and do the same with her.

Dealing with an Angry Ex-wife?

Dealing with an angry former wife is not easy and the solution isn't easy either. The first step is to swallow your pride and apologize to your ex for things you may have done that were wrong. She certainly may have wronged you on many different levels, but if you've contributed your share of hurt, admitting this to her can instantly transform that relationship. Why? Because your ex no longer has to "go on the attack" about your faults. You've admitted them.

Once you've taken the lead on admitting your wrongs, the next step is for you to forgive the wrongs that your ex-wife has done to you. This step is understandably hard.

But that you've now done your part to get along peaceably with her, you can move forward with a clear conscience. Holding on to her past sins will only weigh down your soul with bitterness. So admit your wrongs, forgive her, and experience the freedom that follows.

Single Fathers Can Fill the Void

The plight of single mothers is often highlighted, but the number of single fathers is also on the rise. The 2000 Census shows that there were 2.2 million households in which single men were raising children, a 62 percent increase since 1990. So, if you're a single father, you have plenty of company. The most important step you can take for your children is to surround yourself with a loving, caring church. The church can help meet your spiritual needs as you walk through this lonely valley. It can also pitch in with much-needed meals, babysitting, and even financial assistance. In addition, it's essential to have proper women role models in your children's lives to help fill the void left by an absent mother. You will always find godly women within a church who are willing to take your children under their wing. So, if you've been neglecting church because it's simply one more thing on an already overflowing calendar, rearrange your priorities to make it the one activity you never miss.

What Do You Say to Children of Divorce?

If your children or other children you know have gone through the trauma of divorce, you may be at a loss for words on how to relate to them. Author William L. Coleman in his book *What Children Need to Know When Parents Get Divorced* has some advice. Regularly spend time with kids talking about the divorce, assuring them that the divorce is not their fault. Allow time for questions, and *always* tell the truth. Try to sit down with your kids as soon as possible in a quiet, nonthreatening atmosphere. They may need to vent. Children of divorce go through a host of issues. You can be the steadfast support they need during this terrible time of transition for them.

What Do Tom Cruise and Alan Greenspan Have in Common?

ANSWER: They were raised by single parents.

If you fear the consequences of single parenting may become an obstacle for your children, you can do something about it.

- Make sure your kids have the tools they need. It may be a tutor or a mentorship program.

- Cultivate responsible behavior. Set up routine chores around the house and reward them for a job well done.

- Give your kids support and love in whatever difficulties they face.

Separation in Marriage

Does separation have to lead to divorce? Many couples believe that the next logical step is divorce. But Gary Chapman disagrees. He says separation can "lead to a restored, enriched, growing marriage." In his book, *Hope for the Separated*, he tries to get couples to remember their commitments and the dreams they once shared. So even if things seem hopeless, accept the fact that your marriage didn't fall apart in a day and that it will, no doubt, take time to rebuild it. Above all, have faith that there *is* hope. It may take hard work, but marriages can be saved.

Should a Single Parent Mix Family Life and Dating Life?

You're dating someone you like a great deal and want your children to meet her. You introduce her to the children; they like her and all of you start doing things together. Then the relationship ends. This cycle may be repeated over and over again—and that's not good for your kids. Children become attached, and if they have people popping in and out of their lives, they'll have a hard time feeling secure in their relationships. So don't bring someone into your children's life unless you're contemplating marriage with her. It may take some extra effort and planning—but it's worth it to protect your children.

Helping Children Survive Divorce

In his book, *Helping Children Survive Divorce,* Archibald Hart relates the following:

> My parents divorced when I was twelve years of age. That singular event has changed my life forever. Children of the average, hostile dissolution of marriage are indeed influenced by the process, and they are more likely to be different from other children as a consequence. Why is this so? Simply because divorce, while no longer the stigma it once was, is not a small thing in a child's experience. But children of divorce are not always irrevocably damaged or emotionally tarnished. Everything depends on how the divorced parents behave and how they help their children adjust to the marriage dissolution.

Talking Back

Breathing. Eating. Talking back—all of these come very naturally for children. If you have a child who's always talking back and never quite accepts your authority, you'll have to walk a fine line. After you make a decision, you shouldn't have to keep explaining yourself over and over to your child. At the same time, you want to afford a platform (a little platform) to explain why he or she might disagree with you. There are times when you get the "But Dad." This response provides an opportune time for your child to back up why he or she disagrees with you, but not every time. Listen thoughtfully. Then, if your child hasn't convinced you, tell him or her, "I'm sorry, but my decision stands." Any talking back from your child after that should result in discipline.

Being Truly Successful as a Dad Is to Have a Family Vision

Here's a working definition of a family vision:
To Live My Life Deliberately so as to Encourage, Prompt, and Foster Spiritual, Emotional, Mental, and Physical Growth in My Spouse and Children.

Sounds pretty good, doesn't it? But how in the world does a dad do that? Just as in the business world, you need a strategic plan to help you reach your vision. And while ALL-PRO DAD can't write one specifically for you, we can give you some ideas. That will be our focus over the next couple of days. For a free information sheet on crafting a family vision and strategic plan, visit http://www.allprodad.com/5truesuccess.asp.

Strategies

You need strategies to realize your family vision. Here's an example:

"To lead by example—to demonstrate a consistent pattern of self-sacrifice for my spouse and children. This includes the deliberate putting aside of selfish interests for the good of my family and understanding that the rewards of doing so will far outweigh the slight sacrifice."

Another strategy might be:

"To actively engage my kids' worlds—this includes deliberate steps to listen to and watch what my kids are listening to and watching and to get to know my children's friends. I know many things in our society encourage kids to rebel and behave wrongly, so I will take steps to limit this influence and instead pour into my children good and pure things."

For other great example strategies, visit http://www.allprodad.com/5truesuccess.asp for a free info sheet.

Making Your Own Family Vision and Strategies

You now have some good ideas about how to successfully craft a family vision and strategy. Now it's your turn. We've created a free interactive family vision and strategy chart that you can fill out, print, and put in a prominent location in your home. Put it in a place where it will serve as a constant reminder for you and your household. Visit http://www.allprodad.com/familyvision.htm to get started.

Harmful Friendships

Does your child have a friend you don't approve of? Perhaps it's the way your child's friend talks or influences your children to get into trouble. How do you handle it? If you flat-out tell your child he or she may not be involved with a certain friend, you could have quite a tense situation on your hands. Instead, as a first step, explain to your child your concerns about their friend. Then, if you haven't already offered, have that friend over to your house so you can make a more informed judgment about him or her. If you're still uncomfortable with your child's friend and have legitimate reasons for that feeling, then you as a parent must intervene to keep your children from potential harm.

The Hypocrisy of Eminem

Eminem is both a top male performer and a profane white rapper/singer. His albums have topped the American Music best-selling charts. Yet, he produces special, profanity-free versions of his recordings for his daughter, Halie.

If he doesn't think his type of music is appropriate for his child, it makes you wonder why he and many others in the music industry think it's fine to market it to our children. Just another example of why a dad needs to stay on top of what his kids listen to and watch. The entertainment industry certainly won't.

It's Not a Herculean Feat

It's not too much trouble. In fact, it's only two simple words: "Thank you." It's amazing how two little words can mean so much to your wife who's spent the day dealing with all the stresses of family and work life. It means so much to your kids, who carry out your instructions or go above and beyond what they're asked to do. Expressing thanks makes people feel appreciated—and that's what a father and husband should want to do.

So make gratitude a cornerstone of your daily life—be sure you verbalize your appreciation.

"Husband and dad are the two most important jobs I do, so I strive every day to be the best husband and dad I can be. ALL-PRO DAD is so important because our children do not come with an instruction manual or a playbook. The tools, resources and support offered to fathers through the ALL-PRO DAD website and Play of the Day are special because they help keep men focused on our families and our children in particular."

—Troy Vincent, Defensive Cornerback 2004—Buffalo Bills; 1996–2003—Philadelphia Eagles; 1992–1995—Miami Dolphins

Troy Vincent is one of those men who brings excellence into everything he does. As a football player, he was an All-American at the University of Wisconsin and is currently a perennial member of the Pro Bowl. He has been the NFL Man of the Year finalist and holds the record for longest interception return in NFL history. In the business world, Troy owns all or part of many successful ventures, including Eltekon; Troy Vincent Development and Construction; Essence Hair, Nail & Body Spa; Team 23 NHRA Racing; and Hermann and Sons Beef Jerky.

While these accomplishments set Troy apart on the football field and in the business world, his commitment is first to Jesus Christ and then to his role as husband and father. He's crazy about his wife, Tommi.

"She's an incredible woman, and I thank God every day for her," says Troy.

They met when Tommi was in ninth grade and a good friend of Troy's was dating her older sister. Several years later, when Tommi was a freshman in college, Troy asked the friend about her and they started dating soon after. His persistence paid off as he and Tommi grew in love with each other and eventually married.

Troy is also a dedicated and loving father. He has a daughter and two sons that keep him quite busy. Not only does Troy tackle wide receivers, he also takes an active role in his children's schoolwork, sports, and hobbies. Most important is that he spends quality time with them.

"My kids are amazing," he says. "Each one has his or her own special qualities and traits. I enjoy watching them learn and grow up."

He believes that a father must invest time in his children to raise them to be people of character.

Troy and his wife actively participate in the leadership of several organizations such as the Christian Business Network, Philadelphia Business Leadership Series, Christian Athletes United for Spiritual Empowerment, Professional Business Financial Network, and Trenton Women's Athletics. But home is truly where his heart is. And while Troy excels at intercepting passes, his wife and family are the ones who have truly intercepted his heart.

Nothing Beats Camping

Take a few days and go camping with the family. Sounds like a rather mundane idea, but camping gives you opportunities to fish, canoe, gaze out at the night sky, build a bonfire and roast marshmallows, and so much more. Many campgrounds have hot showers, pools, and game rooms, so you don't have to totally rough it. Some campgrounds even have climate-controlled cabins if you don't want to do the tent thing.

But camping and campfire time is also an ideal time to address a few issues that need to be addressed. It could be apologizing to your family for not spending enough time with them, specifically pointing out things you're proud of about each of your kids, telling your wife how much you appreciate her in front of the entire family, or a myriad of other things. Some excellent campground info can be found on the Internet. Visit http://www.allprodad.com/9campgrounds.asp for a free info sheet on some of the great sites we've found.

Want to Help Your Relationship with Your Daughter Bloom?

The floral industry will tell you that most women love to get flowers. So make a point to send flowers to your daughter. That's right—have flowers delivered to her, whether she lives at home, at college, or even is married and in another town. And it doesn't have to be her birthday or a holiday—just send along a card and tell her you love her. Believe me, it will make her day. So call a florist today, and watch the power of flowers come to life.

Behold the Power of the Garage Sale

Garage sales are cool. Here are a couple of super ideas: give your children a limited amount of money, and take them to a garage sale. Challenge them to get as many "treasures" as they can for their money. Or even better, have them get together with other neighborhood children and host their own neighborhood "bazaar" (or more likely bizarre). Not only can they make some money, but they'll also clean out all that junk that's been accumulating in their closets. And who knows what's lying around in there?

Structure Unstructured Time

According to an article in *Creative Living,* kids need unstructured time when they can choose to do what they want—or to do nothing at all. Like most of their parents, kids today are overscheduled. A University of Minnesota study estimated that children have twelve fewer unscheduled hours per week than they had twenty years ago. Kids need that downtime. Anna Quindlen of *Newsweek* says, "I don't believe you can write poetry, or compose music, or become an actor without downtime, and plenty of it, a hiatus that passes for boredom but is really the quiet moving of the wheels inside that fuel creativity."

Your Last Name

Do you know what your last name means? If you don't, why not find out? There are a couple of websites to help you do just that. Go to http://www.allprodad.com/9lastname.asp. This is a fun way to spend some time with your kids and you'll come to understand the origin and what the root of your last name means. It'll be a great conversation starter with your children, talking about the origin of your family. And get some brownie points with Mom by looking up her maiden name.

Get Assurance about
Your Insurance

Recently a member of the ALL-PRO DAD staff dealt with a burst hot water heater. It flooded his entire house, ruined the carpeting and furniture, and caused some structural damage. As trying as it was for him to deal with the mess, dealing with the insurance company could have been the biggest hassle.

Now certainly not all insurance companies are the same, but you should be well aware of what kind of coverage you're buying. Most homeowners' insurance does *not* cover damage caused by a flood or earthquake. But it usually does cover things like replacing your carpet when your dog leaves little packages on it. Also, many policies cover your goods no matter where you take them in the world. And there may also be some stolen credit card protection. Make sure you keep the insurance contract and cancelled check or credit card bill as proof that you're covered. Take the time to know what your insurance covers.

Adoption

Has the thought of adopting children ever crossed your mind? Without a doubt, it's one of the most enormous undertakings you can ever tackle. For most interested people, it's just an idea that rattles around in the mind or is something sporadically discussed with one's spouse. But why not take the next step and at least speak to an adoption agency? By scheduling an appointment, you can find out what's required of you and get a realistic idea of what adoption is all about. Contact your local or state Department of Children and Family Services and find out how to bring even more joy into your household.

Of Playgrounds and Parents

Have you returned to a place recently you haven't been to since you were a child? A couple weeks ago, I happened to go to a playground near where I grew up. I was shocked by how small it seemed. I remembered it being so much bigger, but of course, then as a child, I was so much smaller. Now that I have grown up, I have a different perspective.

The same principle is true in parenting. Our kids' outlooks change as they get older, especially during the preteen and teenage years. And I mean personal outlooks, not just physical ones. Sometimes we can make the mistake of thinking that our children view a subject such as alcohol or sex the same way they did a few months ago. But that's not necessarily true. So continually talk to your kids about the important stuff so they know that while they may be changing in some ways, your love and concern will always be constant.

Meaning What You Say

Ever heard of tongue splitting? It's the newest rage with teenagers. They literally get the front of their tongues split in half and can then wiggle both parts around—similar to a snake. Let's just say we highly recommend that you don't let your teen do this for obvious reasons.

But do you let your teens speak, figuratively, with a forked tongue? Do you allow them to say one thing and do another just because it's too much hassle to correct them? Letting them do this is far more harmful than any kind of trendy "body art," because we're only as good as our word. And our word determines how far we get in business, in family, in life. Have your kids say what they mean and mean what they say. It will be an important key to their future.

Studying Abroad Broadens Horizons

When your kids hit their college years, you should consider having them study abroad for at least one semester. Yes, it's an added expense for an already expensive education, but as Mark Twain said, "Travel is fatal to prejudice, bigotry, and narrow-mindedness. Broad, wholesome, charitable views of men and things cannot be acquired by vegetating in one little corner of the earth all one's lifetime." Studying overseas (and not just in Europe) will probably be one of the greatest experiences your kids will ever have. Give it some serious thought. It can transform your children's lives.

Working Out Together

How about working out with your teen? It's a great way to stay in shape and will provide ample opportunity to talk. It's hard to just pull your teen aside whenever you think something is wrong with him or her if you haven't been putting in some top-quality and good-quantity time together. But an appointment made with your teen a couple times a week to work out together will greatly enhance your communication and give you the credibility with your teen that you truly do care.

Depression and Premarital Sex

Does premarital sex cause depression in teenagers? According to a Heritage Foundation study, it might. The study indicates that 25.3 percent of sexually active teenage girls said they were often depressed, compared to 7.7 percent of girls who had not had sexual intercourse. For boys, the numbers were 8.3 percent versus 3.4 percent, respectively. The study also said 14.3 percent of sexually active girls had attempted suicide, compared to 5.1 percent of sexually inactive girls. Six percent of sexually active boys had attempted suicide versus only 0.7 percent of boys who had not had sexual intercourse.

There are a lot of other factors to consider in depression other than sexuality, but it certainly looks like premarital sex doesn't lead to the happiness and acceptance teens think they want.

The Cohabitation Myth

A big myth surrounding premarital cohabitation is that it will help prepare for a great marriage. But according to the National Fatherhood Initiative, marriages that were preceded by cohabitation were 46 percent more likely to dissolve than marriages not preceded by cohabitation. In addition, the National Marriage Project states that "no positive contribution of cohabitation on subsequent marriage has ever been found." So it's important that your children know that cohabitation, far from being a great starting point on the path of life, is the road to marital perdition.

The Dating Age Gap Dilemma

Let's say you have a teenage daughter who wants to date a guy significantly older than she is. What do you do? As you know, there's a world of difference in maturity levels during the teenage years. And age difference matters even more when the child is younger. So as a general rule, you may want to tell your daughter that she cannot date someone who is more than a couple years older than she is. Once she's twenty-one, she'll be on her own and will hopefully have the wisdom to discern her own dating age limits. But remember—a teenage girl is still a girl. She still needs guidance in her dating choices.

What Are You Supposed to Do?

Author Steve Farrar in his book, *Anchor Man,* relates an interesting story of a group of appreciative tourists watching a demonstration by the Royal Artillery of the Queen. The six-man team worked with flawless precision. Actually, only five of them worked with precision. One of the soldiers positioned himself about twenty-five yards away from the cannon and stood at attention during the entire exhibit, doing nothing. After the exhibition, one of the tourists asked the staff officer to explain the duty of the man standing off to the side.

"He's number six," came the reply.

"Yes, but what does he do?"

"He stands at attention."

"Yes, I know, but *why* does he stand at attention?"

No one knew why number six stood at attention. None of the other five knew, the man himself didn't know, and even the commanding officer didn't know.

After many hours of research through old training manuals, it became clear what number six was to do. He was to hold the horses.

Why was number six standing at attention? Because he was appointed to do so. Did he have any idea why? No.

There are too many husbands and fathers today who are in the same situation. So how do you find out what you're supposed to do as a dad? Start with "Ten Ways to Be a Better Dad" by visiting http://www.allprodad.com/10ways.asp.

All Parents Are Donors

While science is certainly sketchy on this, some recipients of organ transplants claim that once they received their new organ, they began having the dreams, attitudes, and emotions of their donor. We'll leave the psychologists to figure that out, but needless to say it's a great illustration of what a father means to a child.

You see, part of you dwells in your child. Not just the same color eyes or curly hair, but your emotional and mental makeup. You have a direct influence on the dreams, attitudes, and emotions of your kids because you can understand them better and connect with them in ways no one else on the planet can—if you'll make the time. What have you done this week to further your kids' dreams or lessen their fears? Time will tell.

Actor Bruce Willis on Being a Father

Bruce on being a father stated, "I gained the world. I have so much more love in my life right now—love that I give and love that I receive. It's amazing. I sound like a walking ad for fatherhood, but it's a pretty cool thing."

Yes, the sense of love a father experiences dies pretty hard. In fact, it never dies at all. And it's better than anything Hollywood could ever offer us.

Heroic Men

In the book, *The Bounty*, Caroline Alexander retraces the story of the mutiny on *The Bounty*—an English ship that sailed to Tahiti a few hundred years ago. One question that struck me as I read the book is why would men climb aboard an oversized rattrap and sail 3,000 miles exposing themselves to blistering heat, frigid cold, scurvy, seasickness, dangerous islanders, and just about every virus known to humankind. They slept in an area no bigger than an office desk and would go months without fresh food or standing on dry land. What motivated them? Was it gold? Perhaps. Was it personal glory? Maybe. Whatever the reason, they had heroic blood surging through their veins.

If storms threaten to encircle your family, it's possible to be valiantly courageous in the even the toughest of times. With prayer, honor, and self-discipline, you can rise above the tempest. It will take everything you have, but stick it out. You can do it! Glory awaits you!

Think of Midlife as "Halftime"

So what if you're in a midlife crisis? There's hope. In the book *Game Plan*, author Bob Buford says a great first step for coping is realizing that your best years may very well be ahead of you. In addition, no matter what situation you're in, you have the opportunity to change things for the better. And the dread of getting older can dissipate with the right outlook. As General Douglas MacArthur said, "A man doesn't grow old because he has lived a certain number of years—he grows old when he deserts his ideals. The years may wrinkle his skin, but deserting his ideals wrinkles his soul. . . . You will remain young as long as you are open to what is beautiful, good, and great."

A Legendary Golfer Overcame a Very Difficult Handicap

Professional golfer Ben Hogan struggled with adversity all his life. On February 13, 1922, his father committed suicide. Nine-year-old Ben was in the house when his father took his life. When Ben was twelve, he started to caddy at a local country club in spite of the frequent hazing he experienced. But his biggest challenge came on February 2, 1949, when he threw himself upon his wife to shield her from an oncoming bus. Hogan suffered a broken collarbone, ankle, pelvis, and ribs. Many thought he would never play golf again. But sixteen months later, he won the U.S. Open at Merion, near Philadelphia. And while hoisting the trophy, he saw the reflection of his wife and was reminded of his greatest achievement—marrying her.

Profiles of an Alleged Killer

Newsweek did a story on Lee Malvo, the eighteen-year-old convicted of having a role in the sniper shootings of twenty-one people in the United States during January, 2003. The writer stated, "The more perplexing question is how a boy allegedly became a cold-blooded assassin before he even became a man. The simplest answer may come from Malvo's aunt Marie Lawrence, who described her family's curse. 'We don't know what is father love,' she told Newsweek."

If there is one common characteristic of murderers, it's that if they have a relationship at all with their father, it's a terrible one. One chaplain on death row noted that all the inmates he counsels hate their fathers. Statistics don't lie about the importance of dads in their children's lives. It is literally a matter of life and death.

A Compliment a Day

Many, many married couples never compliment each other on anything. Every time they talk to one another, it's to criticize or simply to pass on information. This isn't how love is supposed to be. How often do you encourage your wife, telling her she's a great mother or bragging about how good she looks in her favorite sweater? Make a mental note to compliment her at least once every day on something different. You'll find the whole tone of your conversations with her will begin to change, and as a result, your marriage will experience a rekindling of affection.

A Great Romantic Idea

Take off an hour or two early from work and surprise your wife by making dinner (and not frozen waffles). Of course you'll need the obligatory candles and flower centerpiece. But some other creative ideas might be putting a little booklet together of pictures of you two from the newlywed stage until now. Or you could gather the pictures together and have a video made for you two to watch on television. Put a little thought into it. Your wife will talk about it for months!

What's Your Wife's Number One Need?

Have you ever asked her? Most wives respond that their greatest need is to experience loving affection; and this does not just mean sexual. It means hugs, kisses, holding hands, and snuggling as well as telling her, "I love you." It means that your wife wants to be loved and cherished.

Another need wives have is to feel secure. This isn't limited to financial security, but also marriage and parental security—knowing you're committed to being the best husband and father you can be.

Talk to your princess and see if she's getting enough affection and security. With these two arrows in your marital quiver, you'll be able to hit the target of relational bliss.

You Should Check Out Checking In

If you're like most men, you'll see your wife for a few minutes in the morning and then for a few hours in the evening. But what about those eight to ten hours in between? That's a long time to be apart. Why not regularly give your wife a call or send her an e-mail just to check in? It doesn't have to be a long conversation—just see how things are going. It means a lot to your wife to know you're thinking about her throughout the day. And it will make going home that much sweeter.

What's Said and What's Meant

Sociologists have noted that difficulty in communication can transpire even when people speak the same language. One noted example is the differences between American and British speech. When asked what their favorite color is, Americans usually just state "blue" or "red" or any of a number of colors. British folks, on the other hand, are more likely to ask, "Favorite color for what? Necktie? Car? Shoes?" In other words, the Brits tend to be more precise. This difference in communication styles caused some serious problems for the Allies in World War II. And it can definitely cause some problems in marriage—igniting a mini-world war of its own. So pay attention to the differences in what you and your wife say and what you mean. And the best way to do that is to listen to her intently.

Have You Ever Thought about Goals for Your Marriage?

As you well know, goals in the business world need to be realistic and have a time frame associated with them. The same is true for marriage. Set goals such as spending one-on-one time together (at least one date night per week), strengthening your marriage (going through three marriage books per year), and staying within the budget (going over a spreadsheet of income and expenses every month), and you'll find your marriage thriving. You don't need to set a ton of marriage goals—just eight or ten important steps you would like to take to deepen your love and commitment with your spouse.

Is Your Wife Your Best Companion?

Is your wife your best companion? The word *companion* comes from two Latin words. "Com" means "with," and "pan" refers to bread. It literally means "someone with whom a person shares bread." The word heralds back to Roman times when soldiers would share bread with fellow soldiers they trusted. It was a symbol of an alliance against a common enemy. You and your wife must be companions against marital common enemies like busyness, anger, and fatigue. Only by talking about potential problems and coming up with the solutions to these will you be able to beat back the dark forces. It's what companionship is all about.

"I've had to overcome many obstacles in my life to quarterback a Super Bowl championship team. And I've had to overcome many barriers to become a better husband and father. ALL-PRO DAD gives men the tools to circumvent obstacles and become great dads."

—Trent Dilfer, Quarterback 2001–2003—Seattle Seahawks; 2000—Baltimore Ravens; 1994–1999—Tampa Bay Buccaneers

It's an experience like no other. The eyes of the world are upon you. Every step, every motion, every part of your game are on stage for all to see. Playing in the Super Bowl is a feat only a few dare dream. Winning the Super Bowl is unfathomable to most people. But not to Trent Dilfer.

Trent led his team to victory in Super Bowl XXXV and got the championship ring. But this ring doesn't compare to his favorite—his wedding band. Trent sees success as a husband and father coming before any Super Bowl or NFL experience.

"My wife, Cassandra, is the love of my life," he says.

Trent and Cassandra have two daughters.

"Madeleine and Victoria know how much they're loved and how much I desire to be a good father," Dilfer says.

Trent credits Cassandra for helping him become a better dad.

While many know Trent as the Super Bowl–winning quarterback, he also excels in many other areas. He had a

3.9 grade point average in college and earned a scholarship. He's an excellent basketball player and was all-conference at Fresno State. Trent is also a great golfer, having won multiple charity tournaments.

While Trent may not get a trophy for being an all-pro dad, the rewards of this accomplishment are much richer.

Reasons for Rebellion

There are a lot of ways kids rebel, but there are two major reasons. First is the lack of a loving relationship with their father, and second is having morally questionable friends.

As has been stressed throughout this book, it's important not only to tell your kids that you love them, but also to take time out to communicate with them and share in their activities. You simply can't expect your children to turn out well if you fail to show them love by both words and actions.

And you can't be oblivious to their friends. You have to know who your children hang out with, what they do together, and what their friends' parents' standards are. Bad company does corrupt good character. Your kids' friends hold tremendous influence over them—so do whatever it takes to make sure this influence is a good one. For a free article on why kids can become violent and rebellious, visit http://www.allprodad.com/7fivefactors.asp.

Kids Can Get Too Busy Too

Many of today's kids are just too busy. Success-driven parents think they must cram planned activities into every single moment of their children's lives so their children can experience the "joy" of childhood. But kids are not built like that. They need to have time just to play and relax. If they don't get that free, unstructured time, they'll start misbehaving because they're tired and irritable. In other words, they're stressed out. Stressed-out kids will not perform well in school or any of their other activities.

So choose wisely what your kids will participate in. Ask them if they think they're doing too much. Talk to your wife about it. Childhood will vanish from your kids all too soon. Help them savor every moment of it now.

Consider Counseling

If you're really having a tough time with your kids, you may want to consider attending some counseling sessions with them. As a man, you may be tempted to think that going to a "shrink" is a sign of weakness, but in actuality it might be a sign of strength. The value of having a third party present to sort through issues can be invaluable. And if communication is poor between you and your children, a counseling forum may help your kids open up. So don't rule out seeking help if you need it. Many counselors are dedicated to helping families just like yours.

How Your Kids Should Handle a Bully

In dealing with a bully, have your kids make their friends aware of this "bullying" situation. That way there can be a united front—bullies have a hard time getting their way with groups. Also, teach your kids how to graciously stand up for themselves verbally but not get into a physical altercation. And this may include just ignoring the bully. Finally, if the teasing starts getting out of hand, you or your child can let a teacher know in confidence what's going on, and the teacher can be sure to monitor the situation. Bullies like their craft, because it gives them attention. But school officials' attention might be just the remedy for these mini-dictators.

The ALL-PRO DAD Cornerstone: 10 Ways to Be a Better Dad

An ALL-PRO DAD does all ten of the following things and does them well. To read about these points in greater detail, visit http://www.allprodad.com/10ways.asp.

1. Love Your Wife
2. Spend Time with Your Children
3. Be a Role Model
4. Understand Your Children
5. Show Affection
6. Enjoy Your Children
7. Eat Together as a Family
8. Discipline with a Gentle Spirit
9. Pray and Worship Together
10. Realize You're a Father Forever

What Happens When You're Wrong?

Perhaps you lost your temper with your children or missed an event of theirs when you said you would be there. What do you do? For many men, it's easier just to avoid bringing it up and to try to do better next time. But this neglects your duty.

First you must tell your children that what you did was wrong and ask for their forgiveness. This demonstrates your humility and that you value them as a person in that you would seek their forgiveness.

Second, you should tell them what you should have done and why. If you were late to their event, tell them you should have planned better. That helps them understand how to address wrongs and make them right.

Third, tell them you'll do your best not to do it again in the future. This assures your children that you're committed to continually becoming a better father.

Protect Your Children from Your Anxieties

Do you talk about your anxieties in front of your children? Do you complain about being able to pay the bills next month? Do you fret about how you're feeling? It's not wise to cause unnecessary worry for your kids. Children long for a safe and secure environment, and anything that will erode that in their mind is an unfavorable thing. Of course, if there are legitimate problems, you'll want your kids to know least some details. It's never good to be dishonest. But if you're one of those folks who constantly worries about what *may* happen, try to keep those thoughts and feelings to yourself. Why?

Because little listening ears can hear words that can break little sensitive hearts.

How Can Water Flow Up?

Author Kenneth C. Davis relates a humorous story about his geography class when he was in fifth grade. One student shot up his hand and asked if it was true that the Nile River flowed "up"? The teacher pulled down the world map and stated that it was indeed true, that the Nile flows south to north and dumps into the Mediterranean Sea. Pandemonium then broke out as the students repeatedly told the teacher there is no way water can flow up while she insisted that "up" and "north" on the map are not the same thing. It was quite a scene.

This little story illustrates what happens when kids' curiosities are piqued in geography. Geography is tremendously important for children to learn, because it ties in with history, sociology, current events, and even religion. So when you and your kids are watching the evening news and a foreign country is mentioned, have your children go find the nation on a map. Maybe even have them read up a little on it. The same situation applies when you're traveling in the car. Have your kids follow your route on a map and be able to tell a little bit about each of the states you're driving through. Just another great way to communicate with each other. Want some cool geography web sites for you and your kids to cruise around on? Visit http://www.allprodad.com/6geographywebsites.asp.

Table Talk

Start a new dinnertime rule. Everyone must come to the dinner table and share at least one new fact learned that day. It could be something from a foreign country, history, sports, or whatever. This encourages kids to learn new things and gives them an opportunity to share something unique with you. Give them encouragement after their reports by saying, "That's interesting" or "I never knew that." And you'll be amazed at some of the things they come up with!

A Son for Life

The National Center for Fathering has some great tips for taking care of your parents as they age:

> Talk to your children about their grandparents or other aging relatives. Describe how you plan to assist them, and ask your kids what they could do to help. Also, do some long- and short-term financial planning. Calculate the cost of your own retirement, and make plans for how you'll lend support to your parents in their retirement.
>
> © 2002 by The National Center for Fathering

Set the example for your kids on how to care for elderly parents. They'll one day have to do the same for you.

Vintage Base Ball (Yes, It Was Two Words Originally)

Vintage base ball is really catching fire. Men are signing up in droves to play the "old school" game as it was played before 1880. Players don't use gloves, wear funny-looking uniforms, and even use a gentlemen's agreement (players call themselves "safe" or "out"). In fact, before 1880, if a fielder caught the ball after it already bounced once, the hitter was still out. Why is vintage baseball so popular? It could be that we're yearning for simpler times and true heroes.

But you know what *hasn't* changed? The fact that you and your children can grab a ball and play catch anytime, anywhere. Some of the fondest memories men have is when their fathers took them out in the backyard or to a local Little League field and shagged flies. And while the game of baseball has changed, using the game to spend time with your kids will always be vintage.

"Dad's Day"

When Indianapolis resident Bill Bissmeyer lost his son to a virus, he wanted to do something lasting to encourage dads and their children to spend more time together. So he came up with this simple idea for his community— setting aside one day a month for fathers and children to meet for breakfast. And it worked. The concept was so popular that within a year's time, one thousand dads and their kids were meeting in separate breakfast groups all around Indianapolis. Something so simple became so noble. And we invite you to do the same. You can start an ALL-PRO DAD's Day group wherever you are. Simply visit http://www.allprodad.com/dadsday.asp to find out how.

Prescreen Movies and Video Rentals

Are you worried about what your kids are seeing at the movies or what kinds of videos they're renting? Are you unsure what to let your kids watch and what to protect them from? Then put the power of the Internet to work for you. There are many marvelous web sites that inform parents about what kinds of objectionable content is in a movie and how often it occurs. Then you can decide whether you want your children to see that movie or not. So do a little research and find a movie review website that meets your needs. It will give you the information you want to make the right decisions.

It's Not Just How Long They Watch, But What They Watch

When you have your kids' television time under control, it's also important that they know what they can and can't watch with that time. Have them submit their TV wish list to you ahead of time so you can approve or disapprove of the shows they wish to view. Once you approve certain shows, your kids must understand that they can't deviate from this list. You may want to break shows down into three categories: shows they can watch alone, shows they must watch with you, and shows they can't watch. This all takes effort and can be somewhat time-consuming, but it's a great way to ensure that the values you're trying to teach your kids are not being undermined right in your own home.

Fathers Make a
Healthy Difference

A Harvard Mastery of Stress study found the following results:

In a thirty-five year follow-up study of 126 healthy men randomly chosen from the Harvard University classes of 1952 to 1954, it was found that 82 percent of participants whose relationships with their fathers were characterized by low warmth and lack of closeness had diagnosed diseases in midlife compared to only 50 percent of those whose relationships with their fathers were characterized by high warmth and emotional closeness.

"Perceptions of Parental Caring
Predict Health Status in Midlife,"
In *Psychosomatic Medicine*,
Vol. 59, Issue 2, 144-149.

Just another example of empirical evidence verifying how important a good relationship between a father and a son is to both physical and emotional well-being.

Dancing Away Disease

In a recent article in *U.S. News and World Report,* Bernadine Healy told about an outstanding discovery. Couples who dance together ward off Alzheimer's disease: "Frequent dancing, which demands musical concentration and knowing where to put your feet while engaging in polite conversation, showed a robust 75 percent reduction in the risk for Alzheimer's."

Does that mean it's time for you to bust out in your platform shoes and powder blue leisure suit? Well, not quite. First, it might be hard to dance with your wife rolling around on the floor laughing hysterically. But second, any activities you can do with your wife that require conversation and exercise will do wonders for your health—and your marriage.

Headphone Problems

If your kids constantly have headphones on their ears, you may have a serious situation on your hands. Hearing damage from headphones is more common than from loudspeakers, because many people listen to headphones at higher volumes. And because the headphone speakers are closer to the ear than loudspeakers, more damage is done in a shorter amount of time. So enforce appropriate headset volume. Your children will then be able to listen to you better—literally.

What Are You Doing to Prevent a Heart Attack?

You can take steps to prevent a heart attack. You don't have to sit idly by and wait for "the big one" to come. Visit your doctor on a regular schedule. Don't wait until something breaks down before you darken the doors of a medical facility. Go periodically even if you're feeling well. Early detection of heart problems is your best weapon. While you're at the doctor's office, discuss with him or her whether you should be taking a low daily dose of aspirin. Aspirin can help protect against heart attacks by thinning your blood and making it less likely to clot. Also talk to your physician about proper diet and exercise. These can be lifesavers.

Your family wants you around as long as possible. Give them that privilege.

Turn Off the Weight

Is one of your children a little on the heavy side? Carrying extra weight around isn't healthful for kids. But before you make radical changes in your child's diet, one of the most fattening things in your home could be your television set. When most kids cut back on TV time, they lose weight. Instead of lounging around and munching potato chips, children are forced to go outside and play. And they'll rejuvenate themselves physically and mentally as they burn the calories.

Is One of Your Children Feeling under the Weather?

Some of children's fondest memories growing up are how their parents took care of them when they were sick. Some children will get a milkshake, a new book, a video game, or a new doll to help ease the pain. Whether your child is suffering from a broken arm or the flu, think of something you can do to acknowledge that you empathize with him or her. It can be scary for a child to experience an illness, since it may be difficult for him or her to fully comprehend what's happening inside. So extra tender loving care by you will make a huge difference and will get your child back up on his or her feet and tearing around the house in no time.

Not So Fishy at All

If you're concerned about your children's behavior and have considered putting them on antidepressants, a new study should give you pause. Harvard Medical School professor of psychiatry, Andrew Stoll, has found that eating fish can be just as effective as prescription drugs in elevating moods. In other words, proper diet can do wonders for your children's minds and attitudes. Parents that make sure their kids eat healthfully and exercise regularly are making a direct investment toward the physical and mental well-being of their children. Take the time to feed your kids right.

Homing

Scientists have no concrete idea of how homing pigeons find their way home. Theories range from magnetic navigation to smell, but researchers simply can't figure out how the birds make it back home. Pigeons may be able to measure the dip in magnetic displacement to help them home, but it wouldn't seem to give them such a reliable guide. Scientists have put frosted contact lenses in the eyes of pigeons, blocked up their nostrils with wax, and even strapped magnets onto them to disrupt the polar field, but the pigeons always make it home no matter what's done to them. They simply have an innate desire to go to the place they're familiar with—and they'll let nothing stand in their way.

Do your children have that same type of desire? No matter where they are or what they're doing, are they drawn to the loving sanctuary of your home? Do you provide the kind of environment where your children will flourish? Take a lesson from the pigeons. And when it's time for your kids to finally fly the coop, they'll be ready to create a loving home of their own.

It's Never Too
Late to Be a Dad

If you're a single, divorced, or custodial dad, you have some hard obstacles to overcome in order to bond with your kids. But it can be done. Wisdom, humility, and perseverance are all necessary to connect with kids you may not always be able to see. Remember: Earning children's trust takes time and lots of it. They must consistently see how much you care about them. But there's also a lot more that can be done. Please check out the free information sheet at http://www.allprodad.com/4buildabond.asp to get more great pointers on connecting with your children.

Success Comes
to the Persevering

He weighed 145 pounds but wanted to play quarterback for a big-name college. Notre Dame and Indiana rejected him. Pitt offered him a scholarship, but he couldn't hack the entrance requirements. After he was finally accepted at Louisville and played there during his college career, the Pittsburgh Steelers drafted him in the ninth round. Shortly thereafter, he was let go. He then started working construction and played quarterback for the Bloomfield Rams, a local semipro team who played on sandlots. He earned $6 a start, plus participation in the many brawls that ensued after the games were finished.

He was soon contacted by another NFL team to be a backup quarterback to starter George Shaw. When Shaw went down with a broken leg in the fourth game of the season, this young man's opportunity came—and, seemingly, went. His first pass was intercepted and returned for a touchdown. He then fumbled on the next play en route to a fifty-eight-to-twenty-seven loss. But most folks agree his persistence paid off as he became one of the NFL's greatest quarterbacks—his name is Johnny Unitas. It's amazing how often success comes to the persevering.

Raising Bamboo and Children

Did you know that there's a certain type of bamboo in Japan that flowers only once every 120 years? It's certainly puzzling as to how this plant can keep track of time, but many factors 119 years before it germinates will determine how much the bamboo will bloom. And that's a long time to wait to see the results.

In the same way, children don't always blossom on your timetable. The love, discipline, and instruction you pour into their lives can't be immediately seen. Your job as a father is to prune and nourish your children in anticipation of their blooming. And once they do, you'll see them grow rapidly into patient, loving, and consistent people. The late bloomers often have the most striking and beautiful flowers.

Think You've Had a
Rough Day at Work?

In 1912 while campaigning in Milwaukee, Wisconsin, Thedore Roosevelt was shot by saloonkeeper, John Schrank, in a failed assassination attempt. Determined to still give his speech, Roosevelt proceeded to unleash a fiery oratory with a bullet still in his chest. After the speech, Roosevelt was rushed to the hospital where doctors treated the wound, but deemed it too dangerous to remove the bullet. Roosevelt carried this lead souvenir in his lungs the rest of his life.

Roosevelt embodied superhuman courage and determination. His life story would be a great read for you and your children. Swing by a local bookstore on your way home and see if you can't find a good book about him that both you and your children can enjoy.

The PatriotGrid?

Have you ever heard of the PatriotGrid? It's a network of computers that anyone with a personal computer can get involved in. By using the power of millions of computers across the world, research teams can generate leads on fighting bioterrorism by harnessing the collective memory of all the shared computers. The grid has been utilized in drug discovery projects including the groundbreaking Cancer Research Project and the Anthrax Research Project.

So how does this apply to fatherhood? Simple. When any kind of information is shared and multiplied, incredible results can be realized. There's an unbelievable amount of helpful advice in cyberspace for you to glean as a husband and father. But you need to be tapped in. And you can do this by starting up or joining a local ALL-PRO DAD's Day group. To find out how, visit http://www.allprodad.com/dadsday.asp.

Alexander the Great

Alexander the Great conquered the known world. His empire stretched from the Balkan Mountains to the Indus River. And incidentally, he accomplished all of this while still in his twenties. Alexander the Great put together an extraordinary feat few have ever surpassed. So what was the key to his success? His father hired one of the best and brightest teachers of the day to tutor Alexander. This teacher instilled in Alexander the duty of knowledge and the value of education. Alexander went on to shape world history because of his father's commitment to knowledge and discipline. Without his father's investment in him, Alexander's tasks would have been impossible. And the teacher's name? You might have heard of him—Aristotle.

"I grew up without a dad. So I know the suffering of children who don't have a father in their lives. But I also know that men can break that cycle of neglect if they get the help they need. ALL-PRO DAD is there to provide it."

Steve Largent

—Steve Largent, Wide Receiver,
Member of the Football Hall of Fame 1976–1989—
Seattle Seahawks

Steve Largent always had a vision for his family. Even before he met his wife, Terry, during their sophomore year of high school, Steve vowed that his home would be very different from the one in which he grew up.

Steve was born in Tulsa, Oklahoma, in 1954. His mother was his rock, especially after his father deserted the family when he was a boy. She tried to do what was best for her family but married a man who turned out to be an alcoholic. During those tough years Steve leaned on other male role models, like his grandfather.

"When a child grows up without a father, there's an empty place where someone must stand, providing an example of character and confidence," Steve told the *Connecticut Post* in an interview. "If no one takes that place, a child can live in a shadow all his or her life. But if someone takes that place, a child can escape the shadows."

With the support and encouragement of those around him, Steve did escape the shadows of his life. He went on to play professional football for the Seattle Seahawks and was later inducted into the Pro Football Hall of Fame. Steve is now a politician and strives to do his best to serve others.

But it's the job of "family man" that Steve values most. His children, Casie, Kyle, Kelly, and Kramer, mean the world to him. And he daily tries to fulfill his vow to make his home a place of love and peace for his family.

You Can Be a Knight in Shining Armor . . . or in Khakis

In medieval times, warriors would often wear into battle small trinkets from their women—handkerchiefs, necklaces, rings, or whatever they could fit into the chinks of their armor. They were a walking advertisement of affection.

Recently when my princess was having an especially hard day, I took one of her hair ties and wrapped it around my wrist. Throughout the day whenever I saw it, I'd stop and pray for her. It did wonders. Not only did God work in that situation, but my princess was floored by what I did. And believe me, I'm no Romeo. Give this simple idea a shot next time your spouse is facing huge obstacles. Just take a trinket of hers and keep it visible on you somewhere. She'll be shocked that, even in the twenty-first century, you can still be her warrior-poet.

Public Bragging

Do you brag on your wife in front of others? Not in a way to totally embarrass her, but to let her know how proud you are of her. Whenever you're talking to friends, try to make it a point to tell them something your wife has done really well recently. Perhaps it was the way she helped out a neighbor in need or what a great job she did redecorating the bathroom. Your wife loves to receive compliments and relishes them when you build her up in the presence of others. Incorporate this simple principle into your marriage, and you'll have a wife who is forever secure and grateful.

John Butler Yeats on Marriage

The author, John Butler Yeats, wrote: "I think a man and a woman should choose each other for life, for the simple reason that a long life with all its accidents is barely enough time for a man and a woman to understand each other and . . . to understand is to love."

We couldn't have said it better ourselves.

How Important Is Humility in Marriage?

Humility is the hinge on which the door of marriage swings. Without it, your relationship is most likely doomed. How many arguments have come from your unnecessary ego? A lot more than you realize. So here are a couple thoughts to keep in mind:

First, pride builds walls, but humility builds bridges. Find ways to reach out to your wife even if it means losing a little face.

Secondly, humility is not thinking less of yourself; it's thinking of yourself less. Strive to esteem your wife more than yourself, and you'll find her to always be your number one fan.

Do You Have a Marital TV-Free Zone?

As usual, it's been a hectic evening helping your kids with homework and getting them ready for bed. Now that the house is quiet and you and your wife have a little time to yourselves, the easiest thing to do is slump onto the couch and watch television until you're both ready for bed. But that usually means no communication between you two. The best remedy is to set aside certain portions of the night during the week when you'll turn the television set off and just chat. Maybe play a board game or do a household chore together.

Marriage lives or dies by communication—so set aside the time to foster conversation.

What Are You Saying?

Have you ever heard what you're saying? It's kind of a strange question, but it's vital in marriage. One day I mentally kept track of normal conversations I had with my wife—what I said, how I said it, and what subject I was talking about. I was surprised at how overwhelmingly negative I was and how I passed these sentiments on to her. She had to deal with my complaints on top of all the things she was going through at that time. So, husbands—listen to what you're saying. You might be surprised at what you hear.

Questions to Ask Yourself in a Spousal Discussion

As you're listening to your wife explain a situation or problem, here's a couple great questions to ask yourself:
"How does she feel telling me this?"
"Why is this important to her?"
One of the hardest aspects of marital communication is not understanding the motive behind the discussion. So next time you're not quite following your wife's train of thought, try to figure out where the train is coming from and where it's going. This will help you understand and respond better, rather than just wanting her to hurry up and get to her point so you can take over the conversation locomotive.

Leaving a Lasting Legacy

There's a new trend among environmentalists that will help them save the planet even after they die—eternal reefs. Basically you mix your ashes with cement and get placed on the bottom of the ocean floor to become a natural reef that helps replenish the sea. Those folks are leaving a legacy for all the squids and minnows to enjoy.

So what will be your legacy after you die? Will you be remembered by more than aquatic creatures? It has often been said that the real value of a person is not measured in his or her lifetime but in the lives of his or her children and grandchildren afterward. Legacies don't just happen, though—they have to be earned. And that means making your family a priority. That way they'll have great memories of you to pass on to others. And they won't need a glass-bottomed boat to do it.

Two Different Worlds Collide at the Threshold of Your Front Door

When you come home from work, you're wearing your day—the stresses, the victories, the discouragements, and everything else that's piled on top of you. Behind your front door another world has been revolving—kids misbehaving, solicitors calling, bills piling up, and another quick supper being made.

Are you prepared to cross the threshold of your door into that other world? Are you prepared to leave your own needs outside and focus on what your family needs from you? How you enter your home makes all the difference. Be prepared to give of yourself and the rest of your problems will suddenly be seen in their proper perspective.

Can You Speak Passionately about Fatherhood?

When men are interested in something, they take the time to know the in's and out's of it. For instance, many of us can name all the starting players on our favorite NFL team or all the top drivers in the NASCAR circuit. But could we articulate why we feel being a good father is so important not only for our children but for our nation as a whole? You don't have to be a family researcher to give an impassioned plea for the need for men to be better fathers. You just have to study a little. You'll never know how reading about the issues affecting fatherhood will pay dividends in the lives of men you come in contact with. For a short article on fatherhood statistics and the importance of dads being in their kids' lives, visit http://www.allprodad.com/1fatheringfacts.asp.

Money

Are you driven by money and status? Your gut reaction might be, "Of course not." But do you spend a lot of time worrying about money? Is it a constant source of tension in your marriage? Are you piling up debt just for the sake of appearance? If you answered "yes" to any of these questions, you might need to reevaluate your whole outlook on finances. Money problems are one of the chief reasons families split up. You can't live above your means and expect your marriage to thrive. Saving instead of spending can actually save your family. Remember: Money makes a great servant but a poor master. Choose wisely.

Choose Your Paths Wisely

One day Alice (in *Alice in Wonderland*) came to a fork in the road and saw a Cheshire cat in a tree.

"Which road do I take?" she asked.

"Where do you want to go?" was his response.

"I don't know," Alice answered.

"Then," said the cat, "It doesn't matter."

The point of this scene is simple. If you don't know where you're going in life, then it doesn't really matter which path you take, does it? The same is true of being a father. Sometimes dads will write to us seeking advice on a certain situation. And that's great. But the bigger question is: What is the father's ultimate goal? If you want your children to grow up to be successful by this world's standards, you'll pick one route. If you want your children to grow up just like you, you'll pick another. But a more ultimate goal presses—what kind of person does God want your child to be? The answer to that will make the path choices much clearer.

Our Busyness Is Getting Ridiculous

Niamh Crowe, a speechwriter in Dublin, has found a great new way to bring in extra income—generic eulogies. Customers can log on to her web site and for $29 can buy a written ode for a mom, dad, grandparent, or any other relative who has gone on to the sweet by-and-by. Crowe believes she's offering a great service of convenience because, "people are busy these days, and good writing takes time."

Now there's nothing wrong with getting a little help in writing your own eulogy, but this is what our society has come to—we're too busy to even properly honor the ones who gave us life. And that's sad. Who knows? Maybe by this time next year we'll have drive-through funerals.

Do You Stand Tall on Your Knees?

How often do you pray with your kids? Have you taught your children how to pray? From the time they start speaking, they should be able to worship God. Imagine if children pray from 18 months of age to 18 years old what an enormous difference that would make. It's never too early or too late to start communing with your kids to the Almighty.

Cohabitation: Not a Good Idea

Are your kids thinking of having live-in partners when they get out on their own? According to the National Fatherhood Initiative, annual rates of depression are three times higher for cohabitating couples as compared to married couples. Cohabitating men and women reported significantly more alcohol problems than married or single men and women. Cohabitating unions see more disagreements, fights, and lower levels of happiness and fairness than married unions. And relational aggression is at least twice as common among cohabitators as it is among married partners. So make sure your children understand that cohabitating should never be an option for them.

In-Law Wisdom

As your children approach marriage, here are some do's and don'ts you need to remember about being an in-law.

- Don't give unsolicited advice unless the young couple asks for it, and even if they ask, choose your words carefully. They'll come to you if they think they need you. Otherwise you're just a nuisance.
- Keep your personal questions to a minimum. They're much more apt to come to you if they feel you're not prying.
- Accept your new son-in-law or daughter-in-law as one of the family. Even if you don't like your child's choice in a marriage partner, you need to respect his or her choice and be supportive.

Abstinence: The Only Safe Teenage Alternative

In her book, *Epidemic: How Teen Sex Is Killing Our Kids*, Margaret J. Meeker notes that 8,000 teens in the United States are diagnosed with a sexually transmitted disease every day, and 80 percent of teens who have STDs are unaware that they're infected. So they just need more protection, right? Wrong! Claude Allen, deputy secretary of the Department of Health and Human Services, says the following: "Condoms may be effective in preventing transmission of HIV/AIDS and, in some cases, transmission of gonorrhea in men, but beyond that, they do not protect adequately against other sexually transmitted diseases."

In other words, there's no such thing as safe sex for your teen. Abstinence is the only way to protect them physically, emotionally, and spiritually. Make sure you're clear that you expect them to remain virgins until they marry.

Cash In on Drug Education

How bad is the drug problem today? Check out this visual illustration about the extent of the illegal drug crisis. The Institute of Biomedical Research found that nine out of ten Euro banknotes in Germany had minute amounts of cocaine on them left by abusers who used the euros to snort the drug. Similar results have been found with American dollars in some urban areas. Illegal drugs and their effects swirl all around our kids today. It's in our music, our schools, and even on our money. Talk to your kids about the dangers of using illegal drugs, and do it as quickly as possible. Multitudes of pushers are looking to cash in on your kids becoming users.

Are You Setting Guidelines for When Your Daughter Starts Dating?

Do boys have to ask your permission before they take out your daughter on a date? If not, why not? It's important that you watch out for your daughter, and meeting her potential dates can only help in this. Make your house hospitable for both of them to enjoy being there together. Encourage group dating. Invite the young man to attend family outings with you. If he's truly interested in your daughter for the right reasons, he'll be glad to get to know you. Many fathers panic when their daughter starts to date and either wring their hands and hope for the best or become a control freak, which in the end, only builds up resentment in the daughter. The point is that you must have a good, healthy, and protective relationship with your daughter before she starts relationships with boys, and it will make it much easier for you to handle her dating experiences.

When's the Last Time You Listened to Music Your Kids Like?

You might want to listen to some of your kids' favorite music. If it's shocking or disturbing, why not suggest alternatives? I don't mean pushing classical music on to your son, if he is a rock music fan. But there are wholesome groups making everything from rap to heavy metal. Just visit http://www.familyfirst.net/musicchart.asp to check out our family music chart. You'll find lots of bands that your kids may actually like. The music is similar and the beat's still good, but the vulgarity is missing.

So tune into your kids' music, and then consider the alternatives.

Parenting according to Blink 182

One of the most popular teenage bands goes by the name Blink 182. And while many of their songs contain inappropriate lyrics, their song "Stay Together for the Kids," aptly describes what many children are feeling today concerning the relationship with their parents. Take a moment this week and talk to your kids about these lyrics and how parental strife may be affecting your family. Your kids will be floored that you're such a hip parent, and it will be a great way to get a discussion going.

Do You Have "Internet Rules" Posted by Your Computer?

If you let your kids use the Internet, you need rules. The first one should be that they should never give out their full name, address, telephone number, or school. And if they make a friend through the Net, they can meet him or her in person only if they take Mom or Dad along. In addition, you may want to consider getting an Internet filtering service. This will block access to many sites that are harmful for kids. Your current Internet access provider may have this option. If not, many other companies do offer this technology.

Of course, the best Internet filter is a father who monitors his child's computer activities. So don't let the information superhighway send your kids on a detour. Get in and stay in the driver's seat for all your kids' online experiences.

Boys Raised by Single Mothers

Boys raised by single mothers genuinely have it rough. They're looking desperately for true manhood and all too often fall prey to what's portrayed in the media or what their friends tell them. Unfortunately, many of these young men do not have a stable older male influence in their lives. That's where you come in. Why not take some time to get to know the sons of single moms? You can teach them what it means to be a man of integrity. You can guide them on the issues that specifically affect men. They and their future families will owe you a debt of gratitude for the rest of their lives.

Travel Smart

Thinking about going to see Grandma for the holidays? Not sure you can afford it? Make sure you check out the great deals you can get on airfare, car rentals, and hotel accommodations. Many airlines give you bonus credits/miles when you get a credit card through them. As long as you pay off your balance each month, you can earn free airline tickets just by using this credit card at stores and gas stations like a regular card. Also, many airlines have hotel and car rental partners who, if you use them, will also get you free airline miles.

So check out airlines' websites and find out how you can save tons of money and make tons of family memories.

A Family Website

Starting a family website is actually a lot easier than you might think. A number of free or very low-cost providers will not only host your website, but they'll also give you user-friendly online programs to help craft your own space on the Internet. A website can be great for sending around to friends and family showing your household's latest events and pictures. It's an electronic postcard that can be continually updated.

Going on a Business Trip That Will Take You out of Town for a Few Days?

Why not leave a surprise for someone each day that you're gone? Your wife would love to open a greeting card each day you're away. If you have smaller children, wrap up a few low-cost presents that they can tear open each morning you're gone. For teens, you may want to leave a few gift certificates. Having something tangible for your wife and kids to receive from you when you're not there is a fantastic way to let them know how much you love them and are thinking about them even though you're not with them. You don't have to do this every trip (we wouldn't want you filing for personal bankruptcy), but it's something you could consider on an occasional basis.

Do You Have a Historic Military Landmark Nearby?

Most cities have some kind of monument dedicated to a battle or certain soldiers who risked their lives for their country. This weekend, take your kids to this special place. Look online and find out what you can about the historical landmark, and have your kids read about it on your way there. It's a great and inexpensive way to teach your kids the value of freedom and what it costs to defend it.

Manna Bags

All of us feel a bit uneasy when we're driving around and see homeless people pandering at street corners. We try to instill in our children compassion, yet if we ignore those who are down and out, what message does that send to our kids? And if we do give the homeless money, will they just go out and blow it on alcohol?

An elementary school teacher had an ingenious idea—manna bags. Simply take a large Ziploc® bag and fill it with nonperishable items like bottled water, crackers, raisins, perhaps a small tube of toothpaste and toothbrush, and so on, and put a couple of these bags in your car. You may even want to have an index card of shelter addresses and phone numbers placed in each bag. Then the next time you're out driving and see a panhandler, you and your kids can present him or her with this love gift in Ziploc®. You help provide for the needs of the homeless and get to teach your kids the value of compassion without worrying about where your money might be going. And indeed, you'll be getting the most out of giving to those who have so little.

"The key to being a good defensive player is having the right strategy. You must be prepared to face any and all circumstances that come your way. That same principle is true of being a father. ALL-PRO DAD helps men develop the right strategy to being successful fathers."

—Travis Hall, Defensive Tackle
1995–2003—Atlanta Falcons

There have been many words used to describe Travis Hall, the football player—intense, relentless, focused, and ferocious. But you need a whole different set of adjectives to describe Travis Hall, the daddy. To his children, Austin, Jacob, and Tatiana—Travis is caring, loving, dedicated, and doting.

Travis knows that being a good dad requires the right balance of tenderness and toughness. He developed his tough side while growing up in the rustic town of Kenai, Alaska, about two hours south of Anchorage. He hunted for his food and chopped wood almost every day to keep his family's stove burning. There were days when he had to trudge through knee-high snow to track down wood that was suitable for burning.

That discipline and determination paid off on the football field. He was an All-State football player in high school and dominated while on defense at college. His play in the NFL has been equally stellar. In fact, Travis has more tackles than any other defensive lineman in the last five years.

As much as Travis loves lining up on game day, his first love is his family. Travis is close to his own father, Mark, and wants to have that kind of relationship with his own children. He credits his parents for helping him develop the tenderness needed to be a good dad. Travis is determined to master that tough/tender balance in raising his sons and daughter. And as we've seen, when Travis Hall sets his mind to something, you can count on his getting the job done with excellence.

One Solitary Life

"Here is a man who was born in an obscure village, the child of a peasant woman. He grew up in another obscure village. He worked in a carpenter shop until He was thirty, and then for three years He was an itinerant preacher. He never wrote a book. He never held an office.

"He never owned a home. He never set foot inside a big city. He never traveled two hundred miles from the place where He was born. He had no credentials but Himself.

"While still a young man, the tide of popular opinion turned against Him. His friends ran away. One of them denied Him. He was turned over to His enemies. He went through the mockery of a trial. He was nailed upon a cross between two thieves.

"His executioners gambled for the only piece of property He had on earth while He was dying—and that was His coat. When He was dead, He was taken down and laid in a borrowed grave through the pity of a friend.

"Twenty centuries have come and gone, and today He is the centerpiece of the human race and the leader of progress. All the armies that ever marched, and all the navies that ever were built, and all the parliaments that ever sat, and all the kings that ever reigned, put together have not affected the life of man upon this earth as powerfully as that One Solitary Life—Jesus Christ" (James A. Francis).

Bidding Good-bye to the Night Train

Former NFL player Dick "Night Train" Lane passed away recently, but his story will continue to be told. Lane had fourteen interceptions in a twelve-game season as a rookie—a mark that has stood for fifty years despite the schedule increasing to sixteen games. He had a total of sixty-eight career interceptions and over 1,200 return yards after picking the ball off.

But what makes Night Train so special was how he overcame adversity from the very beginning of his life. Lane's mother was a prostitute, and his dad was a pimp. When Lane was three months old, his mother left him in a dumpster, where he was eventually found by a woman who later adopted him. Pat Summerall once said Lane was "the best I've ever seen." But Lane's life would not have been possible had not his adoptive mother seen the value of an abandoned infant in a dumpster.

Ahhh—The Joys of Fatherhood

One of our all-pro dads relayed the following fatherhood facts:

- When you hear the toilet flush and the words 'Uh-oh'—it's already too late.
- Play-Doh® and 'microwave' should never be used in the same sentence.
- No matter how much Jell-O you put in a swimming pool, you still cannot walk on water. Pool filters do not like Jell-O.
- If you hook a dog leash over a ceiling fan, the motor is not strong enough to rotate a forty-two-pound boy wearing a Superman cape.
- And a six-year-old can start a fire with a flint rock even though a thirty-six-year-old man says they can only do that in the movies.

Sounds like he's got quite a handful at home. We wish him all the best.

Kurt Warner Didn't Change

Warner has twice been named the NFL's most valuable player. During that time he has also won the Super Bowl MVP award and has been named to three Pro Bowl teams. Wow! For a guy who was stacking groceries just a few years ago with little hope of a pro football career, Warner has come a long way. So has all of his success changed him? Nope. Those closest to him and the reporters who cover him say Warner is still the same polite, classy guy he always was. His faith and his family still come first.

So what about it? Have the years changed you? Has success made you arrogant and impatient with those who aren't on your fast track? Have you forgotten your family and faith on the way to the top? Or have your failures over the years made you bitter and angry? Have you focused so much on being a success that you've allowed not achieving it to ruin your life?

Don't let your circumstances dictate the kind of man you'll be.

True Success

Here is Ralph Waldo Emerson's definition of success:

> To laugh often and much, to win the respect of intelligent people and the affection of children; to earn the appreciation of honest critics and endure the betrayal of false friends; to appreciate beauty; to find the best in others; to leave the world a bit better whether by a healthy child, a garden patch, or a redeemed social condition; to know even one life has breathed easier because you have lived. This is to have succeeded.

The Gnome Liberation Organization?

Ever heard of the Gnome Liberation Organization? They're a group who swipe elfin lawn ornaments and leave behind notes saying they're freeing the little porcelain people. It seems folks will band together for just about any reason these days.

We want to give props to all of you all-pro dads. We salute those of you who work hard to provide for your family, play by the rules, love on your wife, and continually mentor your kids. In an age when so many men simply give up and walk out on their families, you've hung in and persevered through the good times and the bad. You've shown the stuff you're made of. And we're proud that you're part of the ALL-PRO dad family. If you're interested in taking your commitment to ALL-PRO DAD further, we're starting Dad's Day groups all across the country to serve men just like you. You can find out more info by visiting http://www.allprodad.com/dadsday.asp.

A Love Ballad from Major Sullivan Ballou

One week prior to his death at the First Battle of Bull Run, Sullivan wrote the following to his wife Sarah:

> My love for you is deathless. If I do not return, my dear Sarah, never forget how much I loved you nor that when my last breath escapes me on the battlefield it will whisper your name.

What an incredible thing to say! Even more incredible is how we men have become so unromantic not only in words but also in deeds. Telling your wife how much you love her and being descriptive about *why* you love her is essential to a healthy marriage. And this love will be the foundation to a healthy and vibrant family.

Conversation Starters for Use with Your Wife

Try out these questions to start some good conversations with your wife:

- What is your favorite memory of our courtship?
- What is your best memory of your mother? Your father?
- What are your three favorite movies of all time?
- What is the one thing you'd like to be remembered for?
- If you had more time, what hobby would you like to pursue?
- What living person, other than family members, do you admire most?
- What is your idea of a perfect night out—or in?
- If you could spend only $10 on a date night, what would you do?

Ask your wife these questions tonight—you might be very surprised at some of the answers you get!

Adjustment Is the Name of the Marriage Game

One of the hardest aspects of marriage is dealing with unrealistic expectations. Perhaps you got married and are concerned that it doesn't seem to be working out the way you wanted it to. We've been disappointed by our perceptions of who our spouse was.

But, we must learn to deal with our spouses the way they are, not expect them to become someone they can't be. And this can help immensely in the daily endeavors of married life.

What Does Your Wife Think about How Good a Father You Are?

According to research done by the National Center for Fathering, mothers see fathers as understanding less about their children's needs than what fathers believe the children's needs actually are. This contrast also showed up in the category of time spent with children.

When dads (with children under eighteen) responded to the statement—YOU AND YOUR CHILD OFTEN DO THINGS TOGETHER:

- 71 percent of the fathers answered, "Mostly true."

When the mothers responded to the same statement about the fathers,

- Only 55 percent of the mothers answered, "Mostly true."

© 2003 by The National Center for Fathering

So, men, get your wife's input on how you're doing as a father. They can provide you clear ways to continually connect with your kids.

Does Your Wife Snap at You Occasionally?

Living together isn't easy, and there will be times when your spouse makes unkind or curt remarks. So the question is—how will you handle it? Will you snap back? Will you give her the silent treatment? Or will you answer in a gentle, nonthreatening way to bring reconciliation to the situation? She may have said something to you that was totally uncalled for. But how you react will either escalate or diffuse the awkward moment. The choice is yours—and an all-pro dad knows there really is only one right choice.

Listen and Learn

There's a saying that God gave us two ears and only one mouth for a reason—perhaps he expects us to speak only half as much as we're supposed to listen. And listening is crucial in marriage. If you're like me, when you're discussing issues with your wife, you're often thinking about what you're going to say and how you're going to respond—rather than just listening to what she is saying. True listening is hard, not easy. But make a concerted effort to "purely" listen. You may be surprised at what you've been missing.

Burnt Toast, Runny Eggs, and Marital Bliss

Do you have a weekly routine of showing your wife how much you love her? Here's a thoughtful idea: Breakfast in bed.

Pick one day of the week when you'll whip her up a little something (hopefully edible) and bring it to her in the bedroom. You should also take care of getting the kids up and ready. This will allow your wife to relax at least one morning of the week and will be a constant reminder that you're there to care for her.

The "D" Word

Ever use the "D" word in your marriage? If you have, make up your mind that you'll never use it again. The "D" word is divorce. It can come up when you're fighting:

"I'm sick of you—I want a divorce!"

Or something similar may come up when things aren't perfect:

"If you do that again, I'm outta here!"

You need to replace a divorce mind-set with a commitment mind-set. You see, if divorce is even an option, you're more likely to consider it. And the threat of it keeps couples from feeling secure.

Excessive Shyness

D oes one of your children suffer from excessive shyness? Does he or she have trouble making and/or keeping friends? Before you invite your kid's entire school over for a party to try to fix this shyness problem, you should make note of a couple of things.

First, your child may naturally be an introvert. He or she may prefer to read or just keep himself or herself company. And this doesn't mean that your child is weird—it may be perfectly normal. Eleanor Roosevelt and Martin Luther King Jr. are examples of introverts who did outstanding work in their lives. Second, encourage your child to reach out to others and take initiative but not to try to pretend to be someone he or she is not.

Finally, to have good friends, your child must be a good friend. This means he or she should be loyal, trustworthy, and empathetic. If you notice your child does not have those characteristics, address those in a loving and gentle way. As an old proverb says, "He who would have friends must show himself to be friendly."

Reconcile

Have you struggled in a relationship with one of your kids? Maybe you've thought, *I'll just reconnect with them when they get older.* Well, chances are that it won't happen. What you're truly doing as a father now is investing in your kids ten, twenty, and thirty years down the road. Animosity and stubbornness have a way of getting built up over time. So if you share some of the blame in a fallout with one of your kids, do everything you can to remedy the situation. Tomorrow is not guaranteed. And neither is a future reconciliation with your children.

Has One of Your Children Been in a Bad Mood Lately?

If one of your kids has been unusually sullen or withdrawn, there's definitely something going on even if they deny it. So how do you break through? *Persistent loving-kindness.*

Keep asking if anything is wrong, and say how much you love him or her and that this love will not go away no matter what he or she feels or might have done.

Negativity

Do you suffer from *WDS*—also known as *wimpy daddy syndrome?* This is the condition of the married dude who's always whining and complaining. He's constantly telling his kids and wife how horrible his boss is, how messed up his finances are, how he's always sick and tired, how the house is falling into disrepair, and so on. Everything out of his mouth is negative. This destroys a family's sense of well-being. The kids feel insecure and unloved. The wife feels she now has to play both roles of a husband and wife. So be a man. Things go wrong. That's life. Be positive. Your family is counting on you!

Spend Time with Your Older Children Too

If you have a little tyke in the house, think about how much time you fuss over him or her. Whether it's changing diapers, tying his or her shoes, or cleaning up projectile vomit, you spend a lot of time taking care of your little one. But have you paused for a moment to think how this might affect your older children? When they see you spending much more time with the young one, aren't they bound to build up some resentment? So make a concerted effort to spend as much time as possible with your older children. And explain to them that although you love them all the same, sometimes the younger one requires more maintenance and therefore a little more time.

Choice of School

Do you know what the biggest factor is in deciding which school to send your kids to? It's not the school's SAT scores or football record. It's what you as a parent believe to be true and how you want that truth imparted to your kids. Passing on truth, which is the goal of education, doesn't just happen. It must be planned. So the question is—what do you want passed on to your kids? And which type of school will best accomplish this? For a free info sheet on choosing the best school, visit http://www.allprodad.com/6gettinganeducation.asp.

Did I Teach Them What They Needed to Know?

When high school graduations take place, many parents are a bit shell-shocked to see their former baby girls and boys now decked with a cap and gown. An unmentioned worry many parents have as they see their kids walk down that aisle is: *Did I teach them what they need to know?* In the end, that's the real job of a parent. Many of the activities that so absorbed you and them while they were growing up have faded, and now they're embarking on a journey that will take them out of your house and into a hostile world. And there can be an uneasiness that accompanies this. So if your kids haven't hit the high school stage yet, here's food for thought—what do they really need to know? And are you avoiding serious subjects just because you don't want to get into an argument? Time is precious. Make sure you use it wisely.

Homer Drew

Homer Drew quit his job as an assistant basketball coach at Louisiana State University to take over the head coaching position at a college in the hometown of his wife, Janet. They could now spend more time together to raise a family.

But that's not the end of the story. Homer's son, Bryce, was talented enough to play at almost any college he wanted, but he wanted to play at the same university where his dad coached. Bryce, who now plays in the NBA, hit a legendary last-second three-pointer to beat Mississippi in the opening round of the NCAA tournament and helped his college, Valparaiso, advance to the NCAA regional semifinals, which is unheard of for a thirteenth seed.

None of this would have been possible without Homer's decision to put his family first. And his decision turned out to be something extraordinary for his career, university, and family.

An Olympic Hero Who Was
All Heart and Determination

Glenn Cunningham was an Olympic athlete few people today remember. But his story is worth knowing. When he was eight years old, a fire severely burned both of his legs. His doctors didn't think he would live. Then when he battled for his life, they wanted to amputate his legs. He wouldn't let them. A few years later, while watching a high school track meet, Glenn became inspired. He wanted to run like them—only better. During his twelve-year track career, he competed in two Olympics, winning a silver medal in Berlin in 1936 and ran a four-minute mile in 1938. So how did he prove the doctors wrong and overcome the terrible injuries he had suffered? As he told Arkansas' *Log Cabin Democrat* newspaper, "To me it was a challenge. Once you accept something like that as a handicap, you're licked before you start."

So if you or your children are facing your own challenges, think about this Olympic hero who overcame adversity on his way to success.

Doug Flutie

He stands at 5 feet 10 inches tall. He was the fourth-string quarterback at Boston College. He doesn't look like much of a football player. But he went on to win the Heisman Trophy his senior year and become a star in the NFL. Doug Flutie accomplished what many thought he could not. But Doug is even more of an achiever as a father. His son, Doug Jr., developed autism shortly after birth. Flutie was not daunted. He has poured his life into his son's development and also started the Doug Flutie Jr. Foundation for other children with autism. This is what makes Flutie a true champion.

It's Interesting How History Judges a Person

Do you know which baseball player had 493 homers, 2,000 runs batted in, a .340 lifetime batting average, and 23 grand slams? Probably not, but you remember his farewell speech. And according to Shirley Povich of the *Washington Post*, "I saw strong men crying that day, in what was mass weeping in Yankee Stadium, and photographers' hands trembling as they recorded the scene of Lou Gehrig's farewell to the game."

Lou Gehrig's greatest legacy was his character and endurance—playing 2,130 consecutive games. The "Iron Horse" had an iron will, and that is what made him a national hero.

Serving Love

Tennis phenomenon Pete Sampras recently retired. But was he simply basking in the glory of being one of the greatest tennis players ever? No. He was beaming about his new baby boy, Christian.

"I adore this little boy—I really do," Sampras said of his son. "He's starting to crawl now. I'm having to work a little more. I love being home with him and taking care of him, taking care of my wife. It has changed my life. It's made me pretty complete."

All the trophies. All the records. All the money. Yet it took his son to make Pete complete. That's the heart of a true fatherhood champion.

"Make Sure Your Wife's Happy"

Asked what the best career advice was that he'd received, Houston Texans' quarterback David Carr said it came from quarterback friend, Trent Dilfer:

> Make sure your wife's happy. Sometimes they get lost in the big scheme of things because so much attention is focused on us; they wonder where their place is. So I made sure I sent flowers during training camp and did all that good mushy stuff.

Not bad advice.

Do You Have an Inspirational Story to Tell?

Have you faced some incredible obstacles on your way to becoming a better father? Maybe you didn't think you would make it financially. Or maybe your marriage was on the rocks. Or perhaps you found out your teen was doing drugs. Whatever the case, your hardships and how you overcame them can be tremendously inspirational to the rest of our fathers. We invite you to share your story. Visit http://www.allprodad.com/fatherhoodstory.html and teach us what you've learned.

"Being a head coach is a big job, but not nearly as big a job as being a dad. ALL-PRO DAD gives men the equipment they need to do their most important job well."

—Tony Dungy, National Football League head coach 2002–2003—Indianapolis Colts; 1996–2001—Tampa Bay Buccaneers; Defensive Coordinator and Defensive Back Coach 1992–1995—Minnesota Vikings; 1989–1991—Kansas City Chiefs; 1981–1988—Pittsburg Steelers

Tony Dungy says that being a father is his most important job. And just like his football career, being a dad is a job that keeps him very busy. Coach Dungy and his wife, Lauren, have five children.

Coach Dungy's fatherhood role model is his own dad, Wilber Dungy. Tony grew up in Michigan and says his father was always there to support him and encourage him. From him, Tony says, he learned that being a good father takes commitment and compassion.

Since his work schedule keeps him on the go, Coach Dungy tries to spend extra time with his children whenever he can. When his schedule permits, he takes the children to school and picks them up, making the most of that one-on-one time. Coach Dungy also has his older sons James and Eric join him on the sidelines during football games so he can share his work experiences with them.

Quite simply, Coach Dungy loves being a dad. He says a good friend gave him some very important advice years ago that he still tries to live by. The advice is this:

"Fathers need to cherish whatever stage their children are in instead of wishing for the next one to hurry up and get here—because before you know it, that stage will be over, never to return again."

"I review my *Play of the Day* and absorb the highlights. Frequently, I go over it with my wife. Little single point lessons have a great effect for refreshing our minds and applying our spirits. Thanks." —Tony

"I am the coordinator of an adult re-entry program in Iowa and I also facilitate a program called Children in the Middle, which is required for all parents who are divorcing, modifying custody/visitation/child support or going through paternity suits. I use *Play of the Day* as a resource for parents, particularly single dads, but I also find it gives me good insight into my relationship with my husband and helps me respect and support his work as a parent." —Sherry

"Thanks so for your staff's efforts in promoting such a worthy effort. I am a single father who very much relies on the information you send on a daily basis. What is nice is that I compare my methods, approaches, philosophies, etc. to what I read daily . . . to measure myself in terms of being the best father I can. You have my undying gratitude." —John

"I send the good ones to my wife through e-mail. Then we talk about them in the evenings. It provides a wonderful way for us to continue growing in our relationship and focus on some issues that maybe we have not yet addressed. Thank you." —Marty

"I use *Play of the Day* in my Sunday School class and at school where I copy them and put them in the mailboxes of young fathers. I also use *Play of the Day* at a correctional institution in the disciple Bible study classes. There are sixty men in the four classes. Ninety-two percent of the men incarcerated there are sex offenders who need a lot of training and thought provoking, action-taking prompting. If I miss a week, the guys say, 'Where's my *Play of the Day?*'" —Linda

"*Play of the Day* has revolutionized the life of my family. I'm a much better husband and father because of this extraordinary information. Thank you!" —Adam

Join ALL-PRO DAD

We hope you've enjoyed reading ALL-PRO DAD's *Play of the Day*. Thousands of men around the world are becoming better fathers by joining our team. How do you become a part of ALL-PRO DAD? It's easy!

First, sign up to receive our free Play of the Day e-mail service. Log on to www.allprodad.com, and make Play of the Day a part of your daily life!

Second, if you have a passion to help fathers in your city, you can become a part of our ALL-PRO DAD's Day. Visit http://www.allprodad.com/dads-day.asp today to find out how.

Finally, give us your feedback on how ALL-PRO DAD has helped you and what we can do to serve you in the future. Drop us an e-mail at info@allpro-dad.com.

We're honored to be a part of your family's life.

FAMILY FIRST

ALL-PRO DAD is a program of Family First. Founded in 1991, Family First is a nonprofit organization dedicated to strengthening families. In addition to ALL-PRO DAD, Family First produces the Family Minute with Mark Merrill—a one-minute radio feature heard by hundreds of thousands of listeners every week. Family First also hosts seminars and creates other family-friendly resources. For more information on Family First, please visit their website at www.familyfirst.net.